DOSSIER K.

C

Imre Kertész

DOSSIER K.

translated by Tim Wilkinson

MELVILLE HOUSE
BROOKLYN · LONDON

DOSSIER K

Originally published as *K. dosszié* by Magvető Kiadó, Budapest, 2006

© 2006 Imre Kertész

Published by permission of Rowohlt Verlag GmbH,
Reinbek bei Hamburg

Translation © 2013 Tim Wilkinson

First Melville House printing: April 2013

Melville House Publishing
145 Plymouth Street
Brooklyn, NY 11201

www.mhpbooks.com

ISBN: 978-1-61219-202-4

Manufactured in the United States of America
1 2 3 4 5 6 7 8 9 10

A catalog record for this title is available
from the Library of Congress.

The conversation that I conducted with my friend and editor Zoltán Hafner over the course of 2003 and 2004 by way of a so-called "in-depth" interview filled maybe a dozen magnetic tapes. A file containing a transcript of the edited material caught up with me at my hotel in the little Swiss town of Gstaad. Having looked through the first few sentences, I set the bundle of the manuscript to one side, and with what one might call an involuntary movement opened the lid to my computer... That is how this book came into being—the only one of my books that I have written more because of external prompting than out of any inner compulsion: a veritable autobiography. If one acknowledges Nietzsche's proposition that the prototype of the novel as an art form was to be found in the Platonic dialogues, then the Reader is in fact holding a novel in his or her hands.

I. K.

In Fiasco *you write: "When I was fourteen and a half, through a conjunction of infinitely inane circumstances, I found myself looking down the barrel of a loaded machine gun for half an hour." I suppose that must have happened in the barracks of the gendarmerie. Why was that episode left out of* Fatelessness?

From the novel's perspective, it was a purely anecdotal element; that's why it had to be left out.

Yet from the perspective of your own life it must nevertheless have been a fairly decisive element…

Does that mean I'm going to have to say something about things that I never wished to talk about?

Then why did you write about it?

Perhaps precisely so I would not have to talk about it.

Do you find it that difficult?

You know, this is just like the interviews with elderly survivors in that Spielberg series. I hate all those kind of statements like "They herded us into the stables... They drove us out into a courtyard... They took us off to the brick works in Budakalász," and the like.

Isn't that what happened?

In the novel, yes, it did. But then a novel is fiction...

Which in your case I know is based on reality. How was it that you came to be in that narrow courtyard at the gendarmerie barracks?

All things considered, exactly as I described in *Fatelessness*. In the middle of the night—I was fast asleep, resting against the knees of the person behind me, and the person in front of me was resting against my drawn-up legs—I wakened to the sound of shouting and sirens wailing. A minute later and I was standing there, in the yard, under a moonlit sky across which successive squadrons of bomber aircraft were passing. On the low walls, drunken gendarmes were squatting behind machine guns trained on the mass of people who were crowded into the barracks courtyard—on us. But there's no point in my telling you this; you can read a much better account of it in *Fiasco*.

Yes, but there it seems that the boy hasn't a clue about the whole thing, about how he came to be there.

That, in essence, was how it was.

Were you never interested in what I might call the historical background to that scene?

Of course, it's just that the circumstances weren't so easy...

The reality, you mean, not the fiction...

I wouldn't draw such a sharp distinction between the two, but let's drop that for now. The trouble was that under the Kádár regime it was extraordinarily difficult to get hold of any documentation—particularly during the Sixties, when I was writing *Fatelessness*. It was as though they were in cahoots with the Nazi past, the way that all documentation was hidden away: one had to pull out the mostly deficient material from the very back shelves of libraries, and publishing at the time drew a total veil over the past. Nevertheless, I finally managed to piece together that what had lain behind my arrest was a gendarme putsch that had been planned to go ahead in late June 1944. The aim of the putsch, in essence, was to enable the deportation of the Jewish residents of Budapest to Germany to proceed. As we now know, once Horthy saw what the outcome of the Second World War was going to be, and bearing in mind the declaration the Allied powers had made that when the war was over, anybody who had had a hand in the extermination of Jews in Europe was going to be called to account, he ordered a halt to the deportations from Budapest, which was the area over which he had tight control. The gendarmerie wanted to revoke that. As a first step, they threw a ring round Budapest one day at dawn and set up control points at the city's administrative boundaries. As you know, the gendarmerie's sphere of action did not extend to the capital: while they were the arm of the law in the provinces, in Budapest it was "the boys in blue." Anyway, the gendarmerie somehow managed to pull in the regular police, and on that day the police arrested all the people wearing yellow stars who stepped over the city limits, whether or not a person had a specific permit to do so. That was how I was arrested along with my companions, eighteen of us, all boys of fourteen or fifteen, who were working at the Shell Oil refinery just outside the city limits.

As far as I know, the gendarme putsch eventually failed.

That's right. Lieutenant General László Faragho, who, alongside His Serene Highness the Regent, was joint head of the gendarmerie, got notice of the brewing putsch in time, and for his part, he concentrated the regular army troops under his command and duly won the gendarmes round to giving up their plan.

But by then they had caught you. Did that also happen the way you described it in Fatelessness?

Exactly so.

So, it was the reality that you wrote down after all. Why are you so insistent on the term "fiction"?

Look here, that's a pretty basic issue. A couple of decades later, when I decided that I was going to write a novel, I was obliged to sort out, for my personal use so to say, what the difference was between the genres of the novel and the autobiography, "memoirs," if only to stop me from adding yet another book to what already back in Sixties had swollen into a library of, how should I put it...

Holocaust literature. Isn't that what you wanted to say?

Yes, that's what it's called nowadays. Back then, in the Sixties, the word "Holocaust" wasn't familiar; it only came into use later on—and incorrectly at that. I've just recalled what it was called back then: Lager literature.

That's a better classification?

Let's not get into considering the point now.

Agreed, but we shall come back to it later on. What would be of more interest to me right now is the difference between fiction and autobiography, as critics and readers alike commonly refer to Fatelessness *as an autobiographical novel.*

Incorrectly, I have to say, because no such genre exists. A book is either autobiography or a novel. If it's autobiography you evoke the past, you try as scrupulously as possible to stick to your recollections; it's a matter of extraordinary importance that you write everything down exactly the way it happened, as it's usually put: that you don't varnish the facts one little bit. A good autobiography is like a document: a mirror of the age on which people can "depend." In a novel, by contrast, it's not the facts that matter, but precisely what you add to the facts.

But as far as I'm aware—and it's something that you have repeatedly confirmed in statements you have made—your novel is absolutely authentic; every facet of the story is based on documented facts.

That's not inconsistent with its being fictional. Quite the opposite. In *Fiasco* I describe just how far I went in the interests of summoning up the past, in order to reawaken in myself the atmosphere of the camps.

You used to sniff the strap of your wristwatch...

Yes, because somehow or other the whiff of freshly tanned leather reminded me of the smell that used to build up between the barrack blocks in Auschwitz. Slivers of reality like that are, of course, very important for fiction as well. But there is still a crucial difference, in that while autobiography is a recollection of something, fiction creates a world of some kind.

To my way of thinking, remembrance is also the recreation of a portion of the world.

But without going beyond that portion of the world; yet that's what happens in fiction. The world of fiction is a sovereign world that comes to life in the author's head and follows the rules of art, of literature. And that is the major difference that is reflected in the form of the work, in its language and its plot. An author invents every aspect of a fiction, every detail.

But you can't mean to say that you invented Auschwitz?

But in a certain sense that is exactly so. In the novel I did have to invent Auschwitz and bring it to life; I could not fall back on externalities, on so-called historical facts outside the novel; everything had to come into being hermetically, through the magic of the language and composition. Look at the book from that point of view. From the very first lines you can already get a feeling that you have entered a strange sovereign realm in which everything or, to be more accurate, anything can happen. As the story progresses, the sense of being abandoned increasingly takes hold of the reader; there is a growing sense of losing one's footing...

Yes. Non habent sua fata libelli—*books do not have their own fate—as György Spiró put it in his memorable 1983 essay, which as it happened was the first major assessment of* Fatelessness *that had been printed in Hungary since its publication in 1975. But that is getting far beside the point; we have digressed a long way from that barracks courtyard. We were at the point where the gendarmes...*

Declared that they had seen us signaling by candlelight from the stables to the RAF aircraft.

You're kidding!

Not at all; that really is what they said. At first I too took it to be some sort of joke, but then I could see they weren't joking at all. If so much as one bomb were to be dropped near us, they would "hack us to pieces"—that was the threat, and it was clear that they could hardly wait for that bomb to be dropped. They were in a murderous mood, most of them dead drunk, like hyenas that have caught the scent of blood. It was a brilliant scene, in fact, and yet it didn't fit into *Fatelessness*. It almost broke my heart to leave it out, but then there you are: that's fiction for you. Remorseless in its laws. But then I managed to salvage the scene in *Fiasco*.

How can you be so... so...

Cynical?

I didn't want to say it.

You won't offend me. I look on my life as raw material for my novels: that's just the way I am, and it frees me from any inhibitions.

In that case, let me ask: What did you feel that night, when you had not yet acquired enough of that... I would not say cynicism so much as irony to maintain your detachment? The irony with which, after all, you came face to face with death? Weren't you afraid?

I probably was, but I no longer recall. What was much more important, though, was a kind of recognition that I managed to formulate many years later in *Fiasco*: "I grasped the simple secret of the universe that had been disclosed to me: I could be gunned down anywhere, at any time."

A devastating realization.

Yes, and yet also not. You know, it is not so easy to dampen the *joie de vivre* of a fourteen-year-old boy, especially if he is surrounded by pals of the same age who are sharing his fate. There is a... an unspoiled innocence about him that protects him from a sense of being completely defenceless, completely without hope. In that sense, an adult can be broken much more quickly.

Is that perception based on your own experiences, or is it something you heard or read about later on?

It was something that I both observed for myself and also read about. Look, let's be frank here. Among the masses of books on the same sort of subject, only a very few are truly able to genuinely put into words the unparalleled experience of being in the Nazi death camps. And it is perhaps the essays of Jean Améry that say the most, even among those exceptional authors. He has a superbly precise word: *Weltvertrauen*, which I would translate as "trust in the world." Well, he writes about how hard it is to live without that trust, and once a person has lost it he is condemned to perpetual solitude among people. A person like that will never again be able to see fellow men but only ever anti-men (*Mitmenschen* and *Gegenmenschen* are the original expressions). That trust was beaten out of Améry by the Gestapo when he was tortured in Fort Breendonk, a Belgian fort that was set up as a prison. In vain did he survive Auschwitz; decades later he carried out the sentence on himself by committing suicide.

It's typical that those superb—terrifyingly superb—essays appeared in Hungarian translation only recently in the low-circulation publication Múlt és Jövő [Past and Future], *and even that was only a modest selection from Améry's works. But to go back to "trust in the world."*

Indeed, and I think that even at the extreme of my own most emaciated state of physical deterioration that trust... even if I was not exactly radiating it, it must have been plain to see. I simply supposed that the adult world had a duty to save me from that and get me home in one piece. That sounds rather funny today, but it really was the way I felt. I firmly believe that I have that childish trust to thank for my being rescued.

Whereas innumerable other children...

...died. Yes, it's not easy being an exception.

Did any others survive out of the seventeen who were taken off the bus with you and later sent off to Auschwitz?

No, they all died.

Did you get any confirmation of that?

After the war was over, my mother placed an advertisement, but no one came forward. In just the same way as she put in an advertisement in the summer of 1944, when I vanished: the parents of children who vanished at the Csepel Island customs post should make themselves known.

Was it still possible for such an advertisement to appear after the Germans occupied Hungary in March 1944?

So it seems, because it did appear. But my mother took on an even odder thing than that. She upped and just as she was, yellow star on her chest, went off to the War Office—I think that's what the Ministry of Defence was called by then.

She must have been a very plucky lady.

She was plucky, to be sure, but most of all, she had no real grasp of what was going on all around her. Her "trust in the world" remained unscathed right to the end. She was a good-looking woman, my mother; she had an elegant dress sense and would let nothing stop her. She might wear a yellow star and board "the rear platform of a tram" as the regulations required, but men would still leap to their feet and offer her a seat inside the carriage. She was proud of the fact that she bore a resemblance to

Anna Töke, who was a famous actress of the time, so it
sometimes happened that passers-by in the street would
ask for her autograph. She was simply unwilling to face
up to facts, to size up the magnitude of the risks. I just
can't imagine how she managed to get through to the
office of some quite high-ranking officer—a captain or
major. "But madam," the major protested, "please! May
I ask you at least to be so kind as to take the yellow star
off your dress..." Needless to say, my mother demanded
that her son be returned, or at the very least that she
be told where he was and what had happened to him.
What's more, the major made inquiries about it straight
away, and Mother was informed that her son and his
companions had been taken off to Transylvania and put
to work as loggers at a timber-forest there; and even if
her mind was not entirely put at rest by that, right there
and then Mother was willing to believe it for the time
being, because that was what she wanted to believe. At
the time people would hold on for dear life to such illu-
sions as they had contrived about the world order being
rational.

*Astounding! But that reminds me of something for which I
have been seeking an answer ever since my first encounter
with your books. Were the Jews of Hungary really quite so
ill-informed? Quite so much in the dark about what was in
store for them?*

I can only speak for my own experiences in Budapest,
insofar as I picked up anything from my immediate circle of family and acquaintants: nobody here suspected

anything, and I never heard of any place called Auschwitz. All Jewish families would listen in secret to the
BBC radio broadcasts—at least until Jews were obliged
to "hand over" their wireless sets, that is—and if they
heard anything that ruffled their optimism, they would
just dismiss it as "English propaganda."

What lay behind that?

There were many causes, both historical and psychological. There is no question that after the obliteration
of the Hungarian Eighth Army on the Don bend—in
the course of which countless Jews who had been sent
there on labor service, to be used in mine-clearance work
on the battlefield, also died—the enthusiasm for war let
up. That momentary relief, in 1943, deluded the Jewish
population, who believed that they were in a privileged
position. Rumours about the shuttlecock diplomacy being conducted by Prime Minister Miklós Kállay went
the rounds, with people saying that "a deal" was going to
be struck with the Allies behind the backs of the Germans. Then on March 19th, 1944, the Germans occupied
Hungary, and at Birkenau they made a start on enlarg-
ing the crematoria and laying a new railway track in
preparation for the arrival of transports from Hungary.
A high-ranking SS officer by the name of Eichmann arrived in Budapest to be greeted with a considerable sum
of money from the Jewish Council. At the same time
they were given a copy of the so-called "Vrba-Wetzlar
Report" or the "Auschwitz Protocols." Rudolf Vrba and
Alfred Wetzlar, a pair of Slovak Jewish prisoners, after

lengthy and very thorough preparatory work, managed to escape from the Auschwitz concentration camp and to assemble a memorandum in which they gave a precise description of what was happening in that death factory. Considerable space was also devoted to the preparations that were under way to handle the consignments of Jews from Hungary, already then, with the preparations as yet still in progress, anticipating the disastrous fate that would meet those consignments. The Jewish Council in Hungary discussed the report and decided not to make its contents known to the Jewish populace of several hundred thousand, whom the gendarmes had in fact already started to herd together into hastily improvised ghettos.

How is the Jewish Council's decision to be explained?

It is inexplicable in my view. I could perhaps give your question the highly paradoxical answer that they wished to preempt a panic breaking out among the Jewish population.

A bitter paradox... What is most depressing of all is that, sadly, it is all too near the mark. So, you had no idea either where that train was taking you.

Nobody did. There were sixty of us in the cattle truck, and not one of us had heard the name "Auschwitz."

That scene in Fatelessness *when Köves spots a deserted railway station through the wired-over window slot of the*

carriage and picks out the name "Auschwitz" from the build-
ing—is that fiction, or did it happen in reality?

As true to life as could be, and yet it also served the novel's fictional structure superbly.

So, in relation to that, no worry crossed your mind that it
might be anecdotal?

No, because I couldn't have dreamed up anything better
if I tried. Besides which, I wouldn't have dared to dream
up something like that.

There, you see…

See what?

The fact that when it comes down to it you do feel bound by
reality; you do set down real life, and lived reality at that.
There's the football pitch, for example. You write in Galley
Boat-Log *that you have a clear recollection of one at Aus-*
chwitz…

Birkenau.

Fair enough! Of the football pitch at Birkenau, and yet you
did not dare to write that in your novel until you happened
to come across a mention of it by Borowski.

In his short story *This Way for the Gas, Ladies and Gen-*
tlemen. Tadeusz Borowski is one of those writers you

can count on the fingers of two hands who in the death camps discovered something important about the human condition and were capable of expressing it. He wrote five or six powerful short stories in such a crystal-clear style and in such a brilliant, classical form that almost reminds me of the novellas of Prosper Mérimée. And then he too committed suicide. But tell me, now, why do you crow so much each and every time you catch me writing some true, actual detail, or "reality," as you put it?

Because you blur reality with your fiction theory. You cut yourself out of your own stories.

There's no question of that. It's just that my proper place is not in the story but at the writing desk (admittedly, I didn't yet have a piece of furniture like that at the time). Allow me to call on one or two great exemplars as my witnesses. Would *War and Peace*, for instance, still be a good book even if Napoleon and the Russian campaign had never existed?

I need to think about that... Yes, I think so.

But the fact that Napoleon really did exist and the Russian campaign was a reality, and what's more all of it was written down with scrupulous precision, with the historical facts being kept in view—that makes the book even better, doesn't it?

Yes, it does.

And if Fabrizio del Dongo, the young hero of Stendhal's *The Charterhouse of Parma*, wanders irresolutely and uncomprehendingly across fields and groves and continually stumbles into cannon and cavalry units, hears incomprehensible shouts and commands—that's quite an interesting fiction in itself, is it not?

It is.

But if we know that he happens to be cutting across the site of the Battle of Waterloo, that makes it even more interesting, doesn't it?

That's right.

Now, if it's something concerning the Battle of Waterloo, that constrains one to accuracy because the Battle of Waterloo is a historical fact.

I see where you're heading, and I appreciate your Socratic method, but let me ask something in turn. You told me what lengths your mother went to once she knew you had got into police custody—and what a ludicrous expression that is in your case! You said nothing, however, about how she came to know what had happened, because to the best of my knowledge you were living with your stepmother at that time.

My stepmother wrote a letter to my mother in which she told her about my disappearance. What a letter, though! The style! "Dear Goldie (that was my mother's name: Goldie), There is an unpleasant piece of news about which I have to inform you…" "Naturally, I made inquiries at once…" The word "naturally," and the various euphemisms, I "filched" from my stepmother's vocabulary and then made use of in *Fatelessness*. A ruinous personality she had.

What do you mean by "ruinous"?

I'm not really sure… There is a sentence in Gombrowicz's novel *Ferdydurke*—I may be quoting it inaccurately, but it goes something like: "Have you ever known the sort of people inside of whom you dwindle in size?" Well, my stepmother was like that.

Which suggests you had a tough time with her.

And she, the poor soul, had an even tougher time with me. I couldn't stand the… the… To be brief, I couldn't stand her at all; her taste most of all. Just imagine, she had this medium-grey, or rather light-grey, two-piece costume, and to go with that she bought a little narrow-brimmed red hat, a red lacquer purse, and red shoes, and she thought that they made her look frightfully elegant. And she would go out like that with me for a walk— "bunk off a little" was the way she put it. It was dreadful; I could have died. On top of everything, she wanted me to call her "Momsie," and my father backed up this fervent wish. Anyway, they tried and tried but no way did it work; the word simply would not come out.

It seems that already in childhood you were highly sensitized to words. In your most recent novel, Liquidation, *you talk about the phobia you had about some words.*

Yes, some nonsensical scheme was attached to language; the pronunciation of certain words elicited specific concepts, but that's not what is meant in this case. Her grey two-piece suit and the red hat and the "Momsie"—for me all that elicited a horror for which I only later found a name; it was an apotheosis of the petit-bourgeoisie at which to this day I still shudder just the same way. However hard they tried, then, I stayed with the "Auntie Kate," because that suited her, though she was a good deal younger than my mother. But let's not get immersed in childhood memories; in the end you'll want to see snaps of me in my infancy.

Just as you say, but let's stay on the subject for the time being. I would be interested to know what your family was like, how your childhood was spent, and so on. You haven't said anything about your father. A woman who was as interesting as you describe your mother to have been would certainly not have fallen in love with just anyone.

Eenie, meenie, minie, mo, falling in love. "What's that?" Géza Ottlik has one of his characters ask in his novel *Buda.* At any rate, my father was in love, that's for sure, and that was manifested most obviously in his frightful jealousy. My mother, by contrast, wanted to get out of the tight family home, her three sisters, her stepmother, and her father, and his struggles with his financial worries in the small place they had in Molnár Street in the

Fifth, the inner-city district of Pest. At that time—and I'm talking about the 1920s—the road to freedom for girls usually lay through getting married. And through work, of course. My mother was just sixteen when she got a job with a firm working as a clerk, as they called it in those days.

You mean it was not a matter of marrying for love?

Look, it's exceedingly difficult for a young child to judge his parents' love life. Because I was their child, the relationship between the two of them took quite a toll on me.

Did they quarrel?

Not all that often, but when they did, like blazes. I have a recollection of a fine summer morning, for instance. By then we were living close to the City Park in the Fourteenth District of Pest, in a roomy and well-aired apartment—it may have been in Elemér Rod, though I don't know if that's still its name today. I must have been four or five years old; more likely five than four, as I have a clear memory of it. It was probably a Sunday, since both of them were at home. They were yelling at each other. What I picked out clearly was that it was about swimming baths: Father didn't want Mother to go to the swimming baths. He probably suspected that Mother had a rendezvous with someone there. What wasn't at all clear was why my father didn't go to the swimming baths with my mother. On account of "the child,"

I suppose—that was me. Suffice to say, Father snatched Mother's white rubber swimming cap and ripped it to shreds. Mother, for her part, got hold of a huge pair of tailor's shears and snipped two gashes in the front brim of Father's hat. I can see to this day his look of astonishment at the floppy hat brim; it was a green felt hat. I screamed at the top of my voice. In the end, Mother went to the swimming pool and Father took me with him to the shops to buy a new hat. Which makes me think it was more likely on a Saturday, since the shops were not open on Sundays.

Do you have a lot of memories like that?

One or two.

But then they divorced later on.

Again it was me who got the short end of that. I was placed in a boys' boarding school as a full boarder.

Is any trace of that boarding school recognizable in Kaddish for an Unborn Child?

I certainly went to some trouble on that score.

Is it something you don't care to talk about?

On the contrary! One is always happy to think back to one's childhood, however rotten and tough a period it may have been.

How far back can you trace your family tree?

That's a good question, only it's something that never really interested me. Well, however I scratch my head, I get stuck at my grandparents. As far as I know, my forebears were ordinary town-dwellers or, in some cases, peasants of assimilated Jewish background.

Peasants?

Why? Does that surprise you? My paternal grandfather may have been Jewish, but he was just a poor farm labourer. Until he committed himself to see the world. Family legend had it that he walked barefoot to Budapest from the village of Pacsa, near Keszthely, at the southern end of Lake Balaton. That would have been at the end of the nineteenth century, the time when many big careers were made. When he was strolling along what was then called Kerepesi (now Rákóczi) Avenue, his attention was caught by an elegant haberdashery, as they called those shops at the time. He took a huge fancy to the way the shop assistants were bustling around the customers and the counters, so without further ado he entered the shop, and within no time at all he was taken on as an assistant himself. His subsequent life shaped up in much the way that fairytale stories of those days regularly do. He married the youngest daughter of Mr. Hartmann, who was the proprietor of the shop (and I know nothing further than that about this great-grandfather), and before long he set up in business on his own account and opened a haberdashery himself. "A posh emporium on Rákóczi Avenue, with mirrors and chandeliers and seven shop assistants," as family legend had it. By the time I got to know him, though, the poor chap was living in a bedsitter on Tömő Street in darkest Józsefváros, in the Eighth District.

Did he go bust?

In the First World War: he put all his money, his entire wealth, into war bonds. He was very patriotic...

You mention somewhere that he Hungarianized his family name.

Yes, my grandfather was originally called Klein, and he Hungarianized it even before the first world war. As to why he should have chosen Kertész, of all names, heaven knows. "Adolf Kertész, Haberdasher. No credit"—that's what I remember a sign hung up in the shop said. But that shop was in Prater Street in Józsefváros, with only my grandfather and grandmother serving the clientele, who were mainly housemaids from the neighbourhood. "Young Ma'am" or "Little Missy" is how he addressed them, and in the days leading up to Christmas he would give them a pair of silk stockings as a present. He kept his Western Hungarian dialect to the end of his days, so I remember, for instance, he would use the word "underdrawers" instead of "underpants." He never visited a doctor in his life, he never took a tram, and he didn't wear a winter overcoat. I could tell stories about him for hours.

Go on, then. What did he look like?

He was a tall, gaunt man; not a spare ounce of flesh on him. He shaved his head bald. He would sometimes bend down his weatherbeaten and always stubbly face in front of me so I should give him a kiss. He was immoderately proud of the fact that he wore size 10 footwear. I always saw him in the same suit, winter or summer. There were times when he had to go round the wholesalers to stock up on wares. In those days the wholesalers had their warehouses on what was then Kaiser Wilhelm (nowadays Bajcsy-Zsilinszky) Avenue in the Fifth District. I recollect there were grey, frosty days when he would tell his wife, "I'm going into town." As I said, he never took a tram or bus; he didn't wear a hat; he would thrust his hands in the pockets of his grey jacket, keeping the thumb sticking out on either side, turn silently at the door, and vanish in a puff of his own breath like a wizard.

You speak about him with such love...

Yes, and the funny thing is I'm surprised by it myself. It seems he had a greater effect on me than I would ever have supposed. Yet we hardly spoke to each other; now I sense that he treated me like one of the more fragile pieces of merchandise that has to be handled with care lest it is broken. I, on my side, was rather afraid of him. In truth he was a rather dour, taciturn man. He would occasionally crack a lame joke. "I know some Latin as well," he would say. "Listen to this: *adduc aqua cingo*. A

duck a-quacking go." You had to laugh over that. He had
only completed the six years of elementary school that
were compulsory at that time. Very rarely, he would go
off to synagogue on a Friday evening, but there were
other times when he would take me to the Turkish baths
in Dandár Street, since there was no bath in his place on
Tömő Street, and for the WC one had to go out to the
end of the outdoor corridor. There was a big rusty key to
it, hanging up on a nail in the kitchen. He never went to
the theatre or a cinema. He and Grandma would close up
the shop and walk home together. Their supper was invariably the same: matzos crumbled liberally into a mug
of milky coffee—you know what matzos are, don't you?

You bet! A biscuit of unleavened bread.

Well, that's what they ate every evening. The crumbs of
matzo would soak up the milky-brown coffee to produce
a sort of pulp of indefinable colour that would then be
scooped up out of the mug with a spoon. After that, my
grandfather would sit by the window so as not to have
to turn the light on, and he would pick his way through
a newspaper as evening drew in until it was dark. They
went to bed early and got up early; a maidservant cooked
them dinner and took it round to them at the Prater
Street shop in a nest of blue enamel dinner pails.

*You mean to say that even with their modest living condi-
tions they employed a maidservant?*

"Serving girl" as my grandfather said. There's no need

to be so surprised: remember, poverty was so rife in the country in those days that it was quite normal for girls to leave home and go into service in Budapest for bread and board and a pittance for pay. I well recall a long string of "Nellies" who served as maids for my grandparents. The dark "main room" had an extension in the form of a lighter annex that they referred to as the "alcove," where my grandfather and grandmother slept in a vast marriage bed, with my father (until he remarried) at the other end, toward a window that overlooked the Botanical Garden, and me along with Father if I happened to be staying with him. There was a separate kitchen, and that was where the Nellies lived. I was fond of each and every one, and they were fond of me. One of them accustomed me to a taste for cigarettes of the Herczegovina brand, which were made of a light and bright tobacco and had a card mouthpiece. We would sit down next to each other, blowing smoke, at the bottom of the steps: I couldn't have been more than five or six years old. It was the same Nellie who said to me one summer morning: "I'll take the young Master off to the butcher's, and there we're going to buy some paprika-spiced bacon rind and pickled gherkins and you'll find out just how scrumptious that is! You'll be licking your fingers afterward! Only you mustn't let out a peep about it to anyone." My grandparents, you see, kept a kosher household, which simply amounted to forbidding themselves from eating any pork product or cooking with pork fat. So, this Nellie was embroiling me in sin, and she watched contentedly as, one after the other, I tucked into the "soldiers" that she sliced off with her own pocket knife and offered to me on its tip. That Nellie must have been rebellious by nature, I supposed, and she did not like my grandfather one bit: "the old skinflint," was how she referred to him, to my great consternation, because I had no idea what I was supposed to do with such a massive secret. There's no question that this confidence caused me an identity crisis for a while, because on the one hand I had no wish to betray poor Nellie, but on the other hand I was, after all, more inclined to take grandfather's side. On top of everything else, she took me off on one occasion to a church service; it must have been some feast day or other, though that's only now that I think about it, because at the time I had not the least suspicion about where we were going. The afternoon was already dark and sleet was falling. My hand was in Nellie's, and she was clutching it tightly; she probably had the jitters. "The young Master will see!" I think we went along the Józsefváros end of Üllői Avenue, and we dropped into a church somewhere round there. I partook in the same sort of experience that I was later to recognize in the legend of Parsifal, because a mysterious door opened up before me as it did before Parsifal. I stepped into a dazzling space where a long row of trestle tables laid with spotless white tablecloths had been set up. Nellie and I sat down at one of these. We heard some music and ate something. A jingling priest in a spotless white robe came. I had no idea where I was or what was happening, but I was transfixed by a peculiar sense of wonderment and rapture; I was turned totally inside-out.

Or else it was your first encounter with a religious experience.

No, I don't think it was a religious experience; mystic, but not religious. Incidentally, I feel the same way about these things to this day: I'm prone to mystic experiences, but dogmatic faith is totally alien to me.

But surely the purpose of religion is precisely to mediate mystery in order that one partakes of the mystery.

You may well be right, because religious feeling in my view is a human necessity, regardless of whether a person is religious or not, whether or not one is a member of a religious community; indeed, whether one believes in god or not.

And do you, for instance, believe in god?

On the spur of the moment, I can't give you an answer; not that it matters, because I harbour a natural religious sentiment the same as others; after all, one feels obliged to be thankful to somebody for this life, even if there happens to be no one who would be able to acknowledge those thanks.

I would gladly dispute that, but let's move on. The...

Forgive me for cutting in, but I never finished what I was going to say about the Nellies. There was another Nellie who was very fond of taking me out in the free air, though now that I think back on it, that was more than likely on account of a suitor of hers. I seem to recall some sort of uniform that would pop up in the background, then hastily vanish before Nellie took my hand to set off home, though I couldn't say if it was a tram conductor's, a policeman's, or a soldier's. That took place somewhere behind the grounds of the Ludovika Military Academy, in Népliget—the People's Park. As we neared the fairground booths, my ears would be assailed from a long way off by the crackle of music coming from the loudspeakers that were slung up from the enormous trees. They would pour out the hit songs of the day, like "In Toledo two times two is four / To be in Toledo you just have to adore...," or "Fine-cut is a top-notch pipe t'baccy / My chum won't smoke anything that's wacky...," and the like. In front of the puppet show there would be a row of rough-and-ready benches on which would be perched a similar audience, many children, too. I was quite capable of watching for hours as László the Valiant beat the Devil about the head with an enormous frying pan, so it was no problem for Nellie to slip away from beside me. My other favourite was Susie Cabbage, who would tell jokes on a tiny stage nearby, but rumour had it that she was actually a man, which rather put me off. That, anyway, was how those afternoons in the People's Park were spent.

What strikes me listening to you spinning these yarns is how it seems to have been a never-ending summer in the vicinity of Tömő Street, except for the one wintry afternoon when one of the Nellies took you to church.

That's an astute observation. And the reason it may appear so, to you as to me, is because over the summer holiday I used to spend half the time with my father, as I have already said, and until he married Katie Bien, he lived with my grandparents. They, for their part, were in their businesses all day long, my grandparents in their shop, my father in his lumber store.

Your mother and father had divorced by then...

Maybe not as yet, but they had separated.

How old were you at this point?

Four or five, but even later on I used to spend half the summer with him up until I was ten, when my father found a place on Baross Street, still in Józsefváros, at the corner with what was then Thék Endre and is now Leonardo da Vinci Road.

And you have no memories of the holiday weeks you spent with your mother?

Of course I do. Mother always took me out of the city to some bathing resort. My strongest memories are of Erdőbénye and Parádfürdő.[1] It's hard to believe now, but those were then well-heeled, upper-middle-class spas with first-rate hotels that after the war were converted into "trade union holiday centres" and other institutions serving functions of that ilk, and then they were run down to the ground. Once, when we reached Erdőbénye, Mother had something still to sort out at the travel agent's, and I spotted the dried-up bed of a stream nearby. I was curious about what there might be there and, broken loose from my mother's proximity as I was, I started to run, then I slipped on a rock and slid down the steep bank into the channel of the stream and the rocks lining it. That limited our diversions, because for at least a week my cuts had to be dabbed regularly with iodine and the dressings changed. But look here, these anecdotes can be of no interest to anyone, me least of all.

In that case, let's cut back briefly to Tömő Street, because you have said nothing about your grandmother.

No, I haven't, but then there's not much I can say about her, poor thing. By the time I came into the world, the youngest of the Hartmann girls had become a cantankerous old biddy. She was fat, hard of hearing, had trouble with her blood pressure and she continually complained either about her health or how they had "come down" in the world, with reference to the "palmy days." Grandfather endured that without a word, even though it must have been most depressing; however, he would occasionally chide her with a "Zelma, you're always groombling" — like that, pronouncing the "u" as "oo." She would sometimes be overcome by bouts of lovingness when she would be all over me, smothering me with kisses, after which, as I recall—children can be horrid—I would wipe my face.

So, let's pass from Tömő Street to Molnár Street and your maternal grandparents.

I never actually visited the place in Molnár Street; I only know the address because I heard about it from Mother.

In what connection?

She would sometimes bring up the subject of her young days; Molnár Street must have been a nightmarish memory for her. It was the crampedness of the space above all that stayed with her like some sort of claustrophobic memory.

Was that where she spent her childhood?

No, that was just a temporary residence to which they pulled back after fleeing from Cluj-Kolozsvár to Budapest.

When was that?

In 1919, after the Romanian forces occupied the city.

So up till then they lived in Kolozsvár. Can you say anything more about that? Do you know anything at all about your mother's side of the family?

In truth, not a lot. My grandfather was a bank official at the Franco-Hungarian Bank in Kolozsvár. He was called Mór Jakab; he was an elegantly dressed, quiet, and handsome man with a silky moustache and a melancholy smile. He carried around with him the pleasant fruit scent of the nitroglycerin lozenges that he had to take for his heart disease and that he kept on him at all times in a graceful little box in a jacket pocket. I never knew Mother's mother; after bringing her fourth daughter into the world she died from the physical exhaustion of childbearing, and Mother never forgave Bessie (the fourth girl) or, in practice, my grandfather for that, because Grandmother had contracted TB and the doctors forbade her from having any more children after the third.

That's sad, but the poor girl could hardly be blamed for that…

That's what I said to my mother.

And…?

Her response was that she also had other bad qualities.

Was she being ironical, or…

She steered well clear of irony; she didn't have a spark of humour. On the other hand, she was deeply attached to her mother and took great exception to the fact that my grandfather remarried, though he did that precisely in the interests of the four girls; for him to have raised them on his own would undoubtedly have been beyond his energy, which was far from abundant.

In this case, unlike with your other grandfather, I am starting to get the feel of a likeable but slightly dissolute male figure.

You are probably not too wide of the mark. Piecing together all the things I heard from my mother, I also formed the impression that in the marriage between the two of them, the grandmother whom I never knew was most likely the dominant partner, only I have such a hazy grasp of the facts... There you are, a person is sick of family history all his life, and then just when it becomes important, he is left grubbing around in an unfamiliar past.

I have gathered from your writings that you're not a great fan of stifling family secrets, or family life in general.

"Families, I hate you!" André Gide wrote. "Shut-in homes, closed doors, jealous possessions of happiness." Yes, there was a time when I thought that the source of all psychological illnesses, and nearly all illnesses are psychological illnesses, was the family, or stifling family life, as you put it: the big, soft, musty marriage-bed which suffocates all life.

But you no longer think that way?

Look, my second wife, Magda, has a son, and he has a very nice wife, and the two of them have a little girl and a little boy...

And that's forced you to take an easier-going approach.

There's no denying it.

And now you regret not having taken a greater interest in the grandma you never knew.

All the more because among the relatives of that grandmother there were a lot of interesting people, one or two of whom left their stamp on university life in Cluj-Kolozsvár to the present day.

Who are you thinking of?

György Bretter, first and foremost, a philosopher and lecturer in literature who met an untimely death and may well have been a second cousin and in any case was almost certainly a kinsman. My grandmother's name was Betty Bretter. Zsófi Balla, the young ethnic Transylvanian Magyar poet who now lives in Budapest, completed her university studies at Cluj-Kolozsvár and was a student of Professor György Bretter. When I brought up the matter of a family relationship, she said that the way I speak, my gestures, my whole "phiz" reminded her a little of György Bretter.

Did you ever try to establish any sort of contact with him?

Never. At first I shared André Gide's opinion, and now I'm too late. As I said, he died when he was still young, and as far as I know he, too, died of TB, just like my Bretter grandmother. Incidentally, my mother also contracted a so-called "infiltrating" tuberculosis, of which she was fortunately cured around the mid-Thirties at the Irén Barát TB Sanatorium in Budakeszi. By then she had long been divorced from my father, but he still took me along to visit her on the "Magic Mountain" of Buda. We got on the cog-wheel railway in the Városmajor, a long way from Tömő Street, then on the way back we went for a walk on Swabian Hill into town. My father loved going on walks.

So, your maternal grandfather remarried, then at the end of the First World War the family... fled, was that, to Budapest?

That was how they saw it, I reckon.

Your grandfather abandoned a sure livelihood, his post as a bank official—there must have been some pressing reasons compelling him. How old was he?

I'm not absolutely sure about that. He would have been about forty years old. It's perfectly conceivable that the bank would have gone belly-up even without Romanian help. I'm more inclined to think that Hungary's loss of the war hit my grandfather a bit too close. He may well have viewed it as a personal failure; he identified with the collapse and lost his footing in the panic of defeat. Of course, that was an unconscious process, but it happened to a lot of people. At such times one bad decision follows another; people give way to mass psychosis and either slip into deep depression or join the crowd in baying for revenge. It's curious that no one in Hungary has properly analyzed this phenomenon, although the interwar period in Hungary in particular—along with

Germany, of course—produced by the barrel-load the sort of psychoses that prepared people to accept the most dreadful dictatorships and the catastrophe of the Second World War.

You say that people in Hungary haven't properly analyzed the phenomenon, but have you read about it anywhere else?

I seem to remember that Sebastian Haffner, a superb German writer and journalist who fled to London from Hitler, deals with the subject in his books.

But I don't suppose your grandfather was among those who bayed for revenge.

All the less so as he was Jewish, and the sharply anti-Semitic line that dominated Hungarian public life between 1919 and 1924 must have been very trying for him, since he had fled from the Romanian occupation of Transylvania to what was referred to as the "mother country."

Did he speak about that?

Never. And anyway, even if he did, he would not have done so to his grandson, who was just a child. To be quite frank, no relation of confidence ever developed between us, nor could it have done, as we saw each other only seldom. It could be, therefore, that everything I have said about him is purely speculative, but I cannot explain the aristocratic restraint from behind which the lethargy of defeat was perceptible. When I was a young boy I regarded that as an extraordinarily moving trait, though I wouldn't have been able to give it a name at the time, of course. At all events, he was not a great intellect; when he went into retirement, out of his own resources and with help from the family he purchased a modest two-room house in Rákosszentmihály,[2] where he lived with his wife, who I only found out later was not my "real" grandma. Every now and again, my mother's side of the family would get together in that small Rákosszentmihály house on a Sunday evening. By then the Second World War was already in progress. My grandfather would gather the menfolk and usher them into the second room and, brows furrowed by concern, his voice almost a whisper, he would ask, "Now then, what's new? What have you learned? What's going to happen?"

I daren't ask "what did happen?"

Both of them were murdered in Auschwitz. From the window of the cattle truck they were able to throw a letter card addressed to my mother: "We've been stuck on a train, we're being carried off somewhere, we don't know where"—that, roughly, is what it said.

Does the letter card still exist?

My mother had it for a long time. I still remember today the downward-sloping two lines scribbled in pencil on the grey-coloured paper.

And how did the letter card reach the addressee?

Some kind-hearted soul must have found it, put a stamp on it, and posted it. My mother was still at her own address, but during the forced "clustering" of the Jewish population she moved into a "Yellow Star" house in Gyöngyház Street.[3] As you no doubt know, before a ghetto was set up in Budapest, there was an ordinance that decreed that several Jewish families were to move in together into single properties. The resulting houses of mass lodgings were then referred to as "Jewish houses" and a yellow star was nailed up over the entrances. I myself was living in a house like that before... how should I put it: before I was "arrested," specifically with my stepmother at 24/B Vas Street,[4] where her entire family "moved in."

Let's go back a little to Budapest before the war. Your father and mother had divorced, and meanwhile they had put you in a boarding school for boys as a full-boarder. When was that?

Around 1934. I was five and the youngest pupil at the institution. I completed the four years of my elementary schooling there. "Let's leap to it!" says old whatshisname in Zsigmond Móricz's *Faithful Until Death*...

Póslaki.

Yes, of course: good old Mr. Póslaki!

Do you like that book?

I was fond of Misi Nyilas, the poor lad. And also of Nemeček and the rest in Ferenc Molnár's *The Paul Street Boys*. And Winnetou and loads more, but most of all C.S. Forester's Captain Hornblower book.

I'm not familiar with that.

Marvellous book! Solace for my sick soul. Incredible as it may seem, the book was published in 1943, right in the midst of the war! I was given it as a present by my governess, Auntie Susie (I called her Auntie even though she can only have been in her early thirties and incidentally the favourite target of my amatory awakening and sexual fantasies, of which the lady in question would have known nothing), who came to the home in Baross Street twice a week to cram a bit of Latin grammar and mathematics into my dim-witted head. I was thirteen then, and the book was a bar mitzvah gift. You know what that is, don't you?

Sure. A coming-of-age initiation on a boy's thirteenth birthday, rather like Confirmation for Christians.

So, it was necessary to pick a rabbi to conduct the service. The done thing for a boy at the Madách Gymnasium in Barcsay Street[5] was to pick the religious instruction teacher, a certain Itzak Schmelczer, who had a silvery moustache and a neat little goatee. I liked his Old Testament stories in which lords of the desert at the head of their flocks meet up and, as a token of good will, slaughter and roast a kid goat. My mouth would be drooling by the end. I thought the Hungarian word for kid (*gödölye*) had such a splendid ring that for a long time I thrilled in its sheer sound without having a clear idea of what exactly it meant. My father instructed me to ask him what his price was for a bar mitzvah. You want *me* to ask? Tell him your father asked you to. I shilly-shallied for days before I plucked up the courage to approach the teacher's desk and ask: Oh, yes, my father said to ask the teacher what it costs for a whatsitsname, er... The world did not collapse around me, and the floor didn't open up before me, as I was half-expecting it would; instead the rabbi responded: Tell your dad that I'll take it on, and the price is a goose. I would have been happier if he had said *gödölye*. And just to be clear, that was 1943 and the black-market price for a goose was a hundred pengő—quite a substantial sum in those days.[6] The bar mitzvah went ahead; the rabbi and packed congregation sang psalms, and during prayers the elders announced aloud the donations that were intended for the synagogue. I personally was present in my dark-blue, braided, Hungarian-style best suit, a so-called "Bocskai" suit. The utter absurdity of the situation was thereby complete, but evidently no one grasped that. Anyway, I didn't particularly want to talk about that...

No, but about the English sea captain.

Captain Hornblower, the commander of the flagship, then of a frigate, and later still of a ship of the line, which participates in maintaining the blockade that was set up against Napoleonic France. He was a marvellous figure: plagued by an inferiority complex, he constantly doubted his own abilities, fell in love with the unattainable Lady Barbara (Susie for me: if she turned her face to the light a soft, ever-so-fine fluff could be seen on her upper lip, which drove me to distraction!)—a quite baffling figure for a Hungarian boy who had been used to the unimpeachable heroism of János Arany's Toldi, John and Matthias Hunyadi, and the protagonists of Maurus Jókai's tales; a fallibly human figure, who in the end wins his fights and is an implacable opponent of usurpers, of Corsican despots, as Napoleon is apostrophized in the book. Only a dunce could not tell that the latter stood for Hitler, whom the Anglo-Saxon powers would eventually defeat, because they had one attribute no dictator could call on, and that was humanity, the ability to admit weakness, which can be a fount of incredible strength.

You called the book a solace for your "sick soul."

Yes. I think that I was dealing with a pretty sick soul at that time, and I don't mean I was tormented simply by adolescence, the usual tortures of puberty. I hated those around me, hated myself, hated my school, I hated anyone or anything; I even hated having to climb out of bed in the morning. I hated even our home in Baross Street. The housing shortage started in Budapest during the war, you know; that was when the partitioning of apartments started, turning a single solidly constructed flat into two or three shoddily built flatlets. Ours, for instance, didn't have a hallway, so one entered by stepping directly from the outside corridor into the living room, and for some inexplicable reason I took this to be a catastrophe that had been visited on us. It was useless my stepmother urging me to invite my friends round from time to time; I feared that they would burst out laughing the moment they stepped from the corridor into the front room. Apart from anything else the room contained my bed—an ungainly piece of furniture that was a sofa by day and a couch by night. My father and stepmother slept in the inner room, where there was a stupid clock perched on top of one of those obligatory display cabinets stuffed with all manner of china knick-knacks. The clock struck once on every half-hour and on the hour it would peal the Big Ben chimes. Sometimes I would awake early and lie there in torment, waiting for the hour to strike. If it struck just once I couldn't tell from that what time it was; I had to wait for Big Ben. One, two, three... six—no, the pig would chime once more: seven o'clock, time to get up! I would cower mutely in bed. Two or three minutes later my father would start calling from behind the door. He would call my name at an ever-growing volume. Master Imre! Emmerich! Emerico! Grudgingly I would crawl out of bed. It was my task to light the gas ring under a kettle of water for the Planta tea. A tough life kids have.

You were going to grammar school by then.

As I said, the Madách Gymnasium in Barcsay Street.

Around the mid-Nineties, when several of my books
had been published in Germany, I was called on by a
German TV reporter here in Budapest, and he wanted,
among other things, to take a look at the "alma mater"
where I had, so to speak, finished my secondary schooling. It was a boiling-hot summer day, during the school
holidays. The school was undergoing some rebuilding
work, and at the top of the entrance steps stood that
singularly emblematic figure of all public buildings in
Hungary: a cleaning woman with a bucket of water in
one hand and a broom in the other. "Can't you see there's
building work going on?!" she bawled. In the end, she
hunted out the head of the school. She wasn't much
friendlier though. You say you attended this school?
You're a writer? What's your name? Never heard of you.
There were all sorts of famous writers who went to this
school and they always send copies of their new books.
Did you send any? No, I didn't. Well, there you are, see!
says the principal. The German journalist, of course,
didn't understand what all this was about and was getting increasingly edgy. "Do you mean to say that people
here don't know who Mr. Kertész is?" he said in German. Too right, they didn't know who Mr. Kertész was;
they didn't even have a record of establishing separate
streaming for Jews. The class registers for the years from
1940 to 1944 had all been lost, in the words of the principal. How odd, I remarked. We departed.

*I have to tell you that in all honesty even I heard nothing
about "Jewish classes." I had no idea that children were separated on the basis of religion.*

A racial basis, in fact. Hungary's first so-called Jewish law was enacted in 1938, and either that one, or the second one of the following year, reactivated the so-called *Numerus Clausus* of 1920, which had been suspended in 1924. What that meant in practice was that institutions of higher education could only accept Jewish or "effectively Jewish" students to the percentage that they represented in the overall population, which as far as I recall was about six percent at the time; in other words, out of one hundred pupils only six could be Jewish. In that context the introduction of Jewish classes in some state grammar schools counted more as an advantage than a disadvantage, however ugly the terminology may sound. In schools that were so designated it was possible every year, from 1940 onward, to set up a separate Jewish class of forty pupils. These were the B stream, as opposed to the A stream, which was filled by children of impeccable pedigree. Now, in order to get into a B stream you needed to have gained an all-A-grade report at your elementary school. So, judge for yourself what clots these people were to set up a class of children who were the elite of the despised race, whereas the supposedly privileged class had to take the bright and not-so-bright alike. Is it any wonder that teachers secretly competed to be allowed to teach Jewish classes?

Did you encounter any discriminatory attitudes against those of you who were in the Jewish class?

To the school's credit, I would have to say no. The only person who had any of the racist sentiments of the

Arrow-Cross Party was a gym teacher by the name of
Csorba. But we're again in danger of slipping into dreary
anecdotes, like frontline veterans (to use one of Jorge
Semprun's expressions), which is something I would
prefer to avoid.

*And all the more as there are barely any literary relics from
that period.*

Indeed, and that is rather surprising. As far as the period
1940–45 goes, I think first and foremost of the volumes
of Sándor Márai's diaries, then the reminiscences that
Miklós Szentkuthy had tape-recorded and later published under the curious title *Frivolous Confessions*, and
along with that Béla Hamvas's *Carnival*… What else?
Would you add anything?

Ferenc Karinthy's Springtime in Budapest.

Forget that.

Tibor Cseres's Cold Days.

O.K.

Ernő Szép's The Smell of Humans.

O.K.

Tibor Déry's My Memoirs of the Underworld.

We can forget that.

Isn't that a bit hasty on your part? After all, Tibor Déry is...

Yes, of course, of course. Look, I'm not setting myself up as a knocker, and I never had any time for literature of the official canon, let alone the Party-approved *nomenklatura*, but I am impudent enough to select my own reading according to my own taste. There was a time when I had a try with Tibor Déry, but that was a long time ago if ever...

That attempt obviously came in the post-war period, and although I would be curious to know what you read then, let's stick to chronological order. You have hardly said anything about your father, for example.

My father was a cherishable, slim, handsome man with Levantine features and curly, jet-black hair that stubbornly resisted any attempt to comb it. He was a fighter who carried on a struggle that was unknown to me on some distant battlefield. He was usually on the point of losing with my mother. Even I must have noticed some of that during the short period when the three of us were together. *Victrix causa deis placuit, sed victa Catoni*—The conquering cause was pleasing to the gods, but the conquered one to Cato, the Latin saw goes. Well, the latter goes for a child as well. The failure he suffered against Mother totally won my heart over, if not my mind, and this ambivalence shadowed me later on as well. But let's stay with my father. On returning home from his daily skirmishes, in the evening he would complain about his worries and his stomach pains. To stand his ground he would have needed to put on a bit of weight. Every now and again he would haul out a billycan of goose dripping that was being kept for the winter. Have you seen the sort of thing?

You mean one of those blue or red enamel cans with a lid that was locked with a fastener.

Blue: our billycan was blue. That contained the goose dripping, which had a pale-red tint from the paprika with which it had been roasted, and there would also be occasional limp onion rings dotted about in it. Father ate the dripping by the spoonful like Genghis Khan. He was also very fond of cocoa, with garlic on toasted bread: that was Sunday breakfast for him as long as he lived on Tömő Street. My grandmother would bring it to him while he was still in bed, and he would crunch it loudly between his healthy teeth. As a boy of four of five, I would sit beside him in the bed and enjoy the sound of his crunching, the way the aroma of garlic would spread around the bed and through the whole room. I would marvel at him in the barber's shop when he had his blue bristles shaved. He would throw his head back and the razor-blade would work all around his neck. He had a huge Adam's apple that would jiggle up and down under the razor; I would hold my breath as I watched to see the outcome. On Sunday mornings he would take me for a walk: we would stroll to the Oktogon and back. Those walks were very dispiriting for me; I would be bored to tears and feel dizzy, dazed by all the passersby, the Sunday crowds of people. Budapest was a truly fine city in those days; it still is today, but then it was clean as well. The elegance of those Sundays! The ladies' hats! The Changing of the Guard up at the Castle in Buda! The promenades alongside the Danube! In springtime Father would take me on a pleasure steamer, the *Sophia*. I would race to grab seats in the "bows." Father would produce a miniature chess set from his pocket and pin the tiny pieces into the holes by their little pegs. At every turn some surprise would be in store, with adventures lying in wait at every street corner. On the Grand Boulevard, the outer ring road, a bulldog man would put in an appearance every Sunday, sauntering stiffly as he led five or six identical-looking bulldogs on a multiple lead, with an identical pipe dangling from the jaws of the identical-looking bulldogs. Odd characters like that existed in Budapest in those days. Sandwich-board men would pass us by with their slowly plodding steps. In a shop window of the Paris Department Store a chef with a white hat tossed pancakes up in the air from his frying pan. He would always catch them and fry them, and they cost only ten fillérs apiece,[7] except that my father would not always have ten fillérs on him. Then I would be most indignant, whereupon he would explain: "I'm stony broke. Business just isn't going well." That would crush all arguments, on top of which I had no idea what he meant: where was business supposed to go from Koszorú Street,[8] which was its normal place?

A timber merchant's, if what you write in Fatelessness is an accurate guide.

Fairly accurate. It was a spacious cellar property in which timber planks were stockpiled in a certain order. There was an "office" consisting of a glass cage at the foot of the steep flight of steps, but in *Fatelessness* I made it sound a bit posher than it was. There I describe the family as very middle-class, whereas we were much more like lower-middle-class, petit-bourgeois. Father was not able to pay for the stock that he held, so he received the planks "on commission" from the wholesaler, a man by the name of Mr. Galambos, who had a lumberyard somewhere in Újpest[9]—an enormous open-air area with wisps of fog swirling over endless stacks of timber, as I saw when Father took me once on a visit. It must have been in the autumn, and the autumn had much the same coloration as Mr. Galambos. He seemed to be made up of the most diverse shades of grey: his suit was grey, he wore a dove-grey hat and, likewise grey, a genuine pair of spats with little buttons on the side. Even his eyes were grey. as was his extraordinarily neat and elegantly groomed moustache. And he always carried on him, who knows where from, a bag of bonbons or boiled sweets to offer one, in much the same way as one man will offer another a cigarette or cigarillo. That was also the way he shook hands with me, like one man with another, without any hint of a condescending smile or gesture of that kind. I rather think he assisted Father in his business affairs, although I know nothing for sure. In any case, my blood would freeze the instant I heard the word "business."

Why?

It had sinister implications. Either it was "not going well," or it was a cause of "concern" for my father—in short, whenever the word "business" sounded that signalled the end of fun and games, and bleakness would take over.

So what part did the man you call Mr. Sütő play in all this?

None at all. Mr. Sütő is an entirely fictitious character who never existed in reality. In reality there was a chap called Uncle Pista, whom my father referred to as "the hand." "The hand" would help out whenever a "truckload" came, or in other words whenever a consignment of timber arrived from the wholesaler and had to be unloaded from the horse-drawn cart into the cellar. At other times the "hand" would deliver to our house the wood shavings that we used to stoke the tile stove, but that's another story that is of no possible interest.

As far as I'm concerned, everything that throws more light on your relationship with your father is of interest. In Kaddish for an Unborn Child you wrote some truly terrible things about him.

One is always unjust in regard to one's father. One has to rebel against somebody in order to justify our tribulations and our blunders. On one occasion when I was visiting Prague...

I'm sorry, but that's just an anecdote. Please don't dodge the question by taking refuge in Prague!

Well anyway, when I was there I saw a photograph of Kafka's father.

So what?

He was a good-looking man, with a congenial face. Now read what Franz Kafka writes in the *Letter to His Father*.

I would rather cite something from your Kaddish: "We are always sinners before our father and God." Then again: "I had need of a tyrant for my world order to be restored... but my father never tried to replace my usurpatory world order with another, one based on our common state of powerlessness, for example." Also: "Auschwitz manifests itself to me in the image of a father; yes, the words 'father' and 'Auschwitz' elicit the same echo within me..."

Enough! Enough! Look, you're quoting from a novel in which everything is tipped on its edge. The narrator is exaggerating, but because this is a novel every figure of speech has to be distorted to fit that exaggeration. On the other hand, if you really think about it, art is nothing other than exaggeration and distortion, and that is the source of family conflicts. Thomas Mann, for one, was severely reproached for his portrayal of certain family members who crop up in *Buddenbrooks*.

This time you don't convince me. My sense is that behind the passages that I quoted lies a bitter truth, genuine rancour.

A person will always bear a grudge against his or her parents.

If that's the case, what do you suppose is the reason for that?

Beyond any specific individual motivations, perhaps because although it is true that the parents were responsible for bringing one into the world, they also set you up for death.

Isn't that just speculative? I don't think many people think that way.

We know from Freud, however, that there also exists a subconscious world.

Allow me to return to concrete aspects. In the piece on "Budapest—An Unnecessary Confession," which appeared in your essay volume The Exiled Language *in 2001, you describe a scene in which you and your father hurried home. Let me quote the passage word for word: "A confused shouting could be heard from the boulevard. Father said we would not go home the usual way but with a bit of a detour. He guided me, almost running, along dark side-streets; I had no idea which way we were going. The clamour gradually subsided behind us. Father then explained that the German film* Jud Süss *was playing at a nearby cinema, and as they streamed out of the cinema the crowds would hunt for Jews among the passersby and stage a pogrom... I would have been about nine years old at the time, and I had never heard the word 'pogrom' before... But the essence of the word was revealed to me by [my father's] trembling hand and his behaviour." Since you have already mentioned Freud, that nightmarish scene surely carries some unspoken meaning, a reproach...*

That observation is not without merit. One's origins are always a complex and mysterious affair in which one starts to show an interest already when a child. Every child plays with the idea of what if... if I wasn't the person they say I am but, for instance ...

A prince.

Or pauper. Or both pauper and prince at once.

Mark Twain's book must have made a deep impression on you, as you also refer to it in Fatelessness.

If we were not analyzing me but you, then it would quickly become evident that you were ducking a question it may well be I have also never fully clarified for myself. You have singled out precisely that passage, which really does have all the essential features: a highly principled father's downfall in the eyes of his terrified son, who, however, continues to be kept well away from the edge of the precipice rather than their looking down together and assessing its depth. The big question is whether my father for his part ever took a look over the precipice. I have no way of knowing whether he had a guilty conscience about handing on his increasingly ominous heritage, or in plain language, for bringing a Jewish child into this unfriendly world. That he never verbalized it for himself—of that I am quite sure, but that would not necessarily have saved him from twinges of guilty conscience, for which he may then have compensated precisely by the show of infallible principle. As a result, I was more, so to say, ordered into my Jewishness instead of won over by argument that that was how the thing had to be. The difference may be small, but it's important. There wasn't anything for me to *shoulder* of my own accord, so I was deprived of any sense of responsibility; the most I could do was show my dissatisfaction, mutter to myself, or dream about a less nauseating situation. In point of fact, I think that was the origin of the psychological conflicts that eventually culminated in the form of Jewish self-hatred, a type that was particularly well known among Eastern European Jews as they rose into the middle classes, with Otto Weininger, or indeed Ludwig Wittgenstein, as typical highly cultured representatives. They are good examples of the fact that philosophical flair in itself offers no protection against misconceptions; indeed, quite the contrary. This is a big issue, and one under whose weight many have cracked up or, quite the opposite, turned aggressive and developed major character flaws.

You yourself, nevertheless, still managed to find another solution.

I don't think so. This has no solution; the problem

constantly follows one around, like one's own shadow. I at most gave in to the temptation to be frank, but for that—if I may be permitted to express myself in a rather extreme fashion—I needed Auschwitz. Could we not find something cheerier to talk about?

That would call for a cheerier C.V.

All in all, I'm on the side of cheeriness. My error is that I don't elicit that feeling in others. But see here: I was able to win intellectual freedom fairly early on, and from the moment I decided to become a writer I was able to treat my cares as the raw material of my art. And even if that raw material looks fairly cheerless, the form is able to transform it and turn it into pleasure, because writing can only come from an abundance of energies, from pleasure; writing—and this is not my invention— is heightened life.

You only reached the pleasure, as you yourself pointed out, at the expense of suffering, and I can now see your rela- tionship with your father more clearly: to put it simply, the relationship was not exactly one characterized by openness.

No, there were undoubtedly things that we kept quiet about in each other's presence: my father about the kind of fate into which he had helped bring me, and I about the fact that I did not accept that fate. Neither of us knew about this; we just saw the result, and that was painful. My defiance extended to everything; a distance grew up inside me instead of solidarity. I have already said that I had no liking for myself in that destructive role; I would much rather have been a pliant but carefree little boy, a good pupil, with a clear conscience, honest, industrious, lovable, but whenever I tried to be that, I would be disgusted by myself. I learned how to lie early on, but I was incapable of self-denial. Now that I'm saying this, I'm seized by an unbounded love for my father: the poor soul, he was unable to grasp why he had such a hard time with me.

You seem to be trying to portray yourself as a devious, bad-tempered child.

Bad-tempered, never; I found it easy to make friends, I was game for any escapade, any laughs. And sneaky only to the extent that I felt constrained to it by my situation. Like I said, I was unaware of my own problem, about which I would now declare pompously that it was an internalization of the Jewish question in semi-fascist Hungary.

Did that "situation" also throw a shadow on your relations with your mother? Or were you able to speak more frankly with her?

My mother had no interest at all in the Jewish question apart from its—how should I put it?—its technical side, and then later on the threat to life. My mother was high-spirited, a true epicurean, and she didn't let herself be bothered too much by a few anti-Semites. Religion as such, as meditation, faith, inwardness, piety, spirituality, and so on, was alien to her. In any event, because she was advised to do so by the people in her circle in the late Thirties, she converted to some other confession—the Reformed Church as best I recall, but that was a pure formality that subsequently, when it turned out that it would in no way give her any protection, she largely forgot all about. She had quite a hard job getting a divorce from my father, because in those days divorces came with a string of onerous legal stipulations. It was necessary to spell out, for instance, if the divorce was being granted on the grounds of the husband's or the wife's fault, and my father insisted on the condition that the divorce was being granted on account of my mother's fault. That in turn meant that my mother had to renounce any rights over her son, and she had to agree to certain stipulations about "visitation," which duly occurred. As a result, I was able to see my mother once a week, and during the holidays twice a week. After the divorce, she lived for a while in a boarding house in Pannónia Road in the Sixth (Terézváros) District, which I supposed was a terribly chic thing to do. Later on, at much the same time as my father took a second wife, she too remarried, a fairly comfortably well-off gentleman by the name of László Seres, who was known to me as Laci or Uncle Laci. He was a stocky, well-dressed, bald-pated fellow, an engaging upright citizen, who, to the best of my knowledge, was the one true love of my mother's life. He was the managing director of some big company until he was forced into retirement by the Jewish laws. Needless to say, I was none too well disposed to him, though over the years that antipathy vanished bit by bit for the very simple reason that he never tried to win me over. On the whole, my mother and those around her handled the embarrassing position I was put in after the divorce a good deal more elegantly than did my father, who— Auntie Kate here or there—emerged the clear loser and did not spare me any of his ironic bitterness. For instance, every week Laci Seres would give me a shiny silver five-pengő piece. "Tell the fat-head you don't need any money!" my father would urge. That says little for his big-heartedness, but it did at least bring me closer to Father—you remember Cato and the conquered one, don't you?…

Would it be fair to say that for you there were two separate worlds that you somehow had to balance?

That's exactly how it was. To make that even more definitive, my mother and her husband moved to Buda and leased a house at the foot of Rose Hill in the Second District. To live in a place in Buda counted as a very genteel thing in those days. Paradoxically, the prospect of war ushered in a building boom, with the empty plots on Convent (now Rómer Flóris) Street and Zivatar Street being built on one after the other. I liked the little modern apartment that my mother and Uncle Laci had on Zivatar Street. The stairway still smelled of new building materials, while the bright kitchen overlooked the outside dining tables of the Nardai Restaurant on Kút Street. Of an evening a discreet rattle of tableware and scraps of laughter and Gypsy music would drift up from the lantern-lit garden. Decades later, when Mahler's

Ninth Symphony had a huge impact on my life, that passage in the first movement where, all of a sudden, a nos-
talgic motif—a Proustian snatch of melody—sounds on
a single violin, each and every time I had to recollect the
Gypsy music at the Nardai Restaurant. And you know,
even today I am convinced that Mahler may have taken
that mood away from one of his regular eating haunts
during his period as musical director at the Royal Opera
House in Budapest. Anyway, yes, you're right, my father
and mother did represent two different worlds in my
life. On arriving at Mother's place from distant Baross
Street, I would usually have to take off my clothes and
put on some more elegant outfit that was more to her
taste. She would have me bathe in the gleaming bathroom, even washing my hair with foaming shampoo,
and in a way that was all the more eloquent, for her saying nothing would give me to understand exactly what
she thought of my father; and that, when it came down
to it, was every bit as painful as having to swallow my
father's cutting remarks.

*So, you were living a double life, and the two worlds were
pretty divergent. Didn't that push you into an identity crisis
of any kind?*

No, and all the less so in that I had no identity; I didn't
need one. What would I have done with one, anyway? I
needed adaptability, not an identity. And anyway, that
double life was far more entertaining than if I had had
to get by purely on the monotony of Baross Street. At
Zivatar Street, by contrast, it was the dominance of Laci

Seres that made me feel ill at ease. He was an intelligent man, and the way I saw it he didn't think too highly of me. I can well imagine, indeed readily appreciate, how discomfiting the child of Mother's previous marriage must have been for him, turning up every week from a foreign world to spoil the afternoon. It was only the two of us, however, who were in the know about my super-fluousness; Mother noticed nothing. It was a bit like a mute alliance between the two of us for the sake of my mother, and that at times led to almost mutual cordiality. It was a tolerable life. I had certain games that I played exclusively at my mother's place, books that I only read when I was there.

How did you come to be at the Shell Oil refinery in the summer of 1944?

In what I might call a quite natural way. I presume you know a bit about the Levente movement.[10] Anyway, at the start of the 1943–44 grammar school year—I was thirteen and in Year 3 then—that still appeared to be just some stupid phooey. Once a week we had to line up in the schoolyard under the supervision of Csorba, the gym teacher whom I mentioned earlier. On these occasions, the boys of stream B received what I may safely call an introductory course to Auschwitz. Not that it was called that, of course, and I dare say that even gym master Csorba was not fully aware of the reality, although he needed to do no more than think through where the logic of his activity was leading to. Allow me at this point to wheel out my favourite Kafka quotation, a sentence from *The Trial*: "*Judgment does not come suddenly; the proceedings gradually merge into the judgment.*" The system of terror in Germany was forceful, whereas in Hungary—even before the German occupation in early 1944—it was simply unpredictable. But the *proceedings* had already started and were steadily moving ahead along the designated route. For the Levente lesson, a B-stream pupil would slip on a yellow arm band that his mother (or auntie or the chambermaid) had sewed for him at home and learned that he was to be addressed as "Master Ancillary Trainee," which he would then discuss in guffaws with his companions as the expression was incomprehensible and truly ridiculous. On these occasions gym teacher Csorba would strut around in some sort of officer's cap: "Trainee Corps, fall in!" he would bawl. The Levente lessons had to be taken seriously because they were compulsory. In Hungary under the German occupation, however, after the schools were closed early for the summer vacation, every "Master" over fourteen who was liable to do Levente service had to possess an officially verified workplace. I had received from the borough council a communication to the effect that I could either pick such a workplace for myself or they would assign one. I elected for the latter and obtained the Shell Oil refinery, and the rest you know. I hope I'm not expected to go over again the story of how I was picked up by the police, the gendarmes, the brickyard...

That is the story of the year that we know about from Fatelessness.

Maybe we should pick up again on our chat regarding the distinction between fiction and an autobiographical novel...

I wouldn't set my heart on it. There's just one question that I would like to ask, but that one in any case. How should I put it, then? To what extent does György Köves resemble the person who you were? To continue that line of thought: to what extent were you, Imre Kertész, helped to survive, or to what extent was it made more difficult, by your sad childhood, that alienated way of life, lacking in all intimacy, on which some light has been thrown by our conversation so far?

A good question, and one it is worth contemplating, although I feel it is something I have always been thinking about. The question reminds me of one of Jean Améry's essays, in which he broods on whether culture, or education, was of any assistance to intellectuals in Auschwitz. He comes to the conclusion that it wasn't; indeed, educated people had a harder time of it in the death camps than did ordinary, uneducated people. Now that may well be true in practice, but—being in possession of that culture—if one thinks a bit more profoundly about Auschwitz, about the establishment and running of the death camp, then one has to concede the necessity of those institutions. Yes, indeed, if you consider one line taken by European history and analyze it with your post-facto knowledge of the way in which, for centuries now, mankind has been thinking and acting, the way in which he has been living, then the setting-up of the machinery for the extermination of European Jewry is no big surprise.

You mean Auschwitz is an inevitable and logical consequence of…

No, I don't mean that: Where Auschwitz starts logic stops. What comes to the fore is a kind of compulsive thought process that is very similar to logic because it leads people, only not on the path of logic. Now, I look for that thread, that aberrant train of thought that coercively passes absurdity off as logic, because once one is in the trap of Auschwitz there is no choice. More than that, we get a rehearsal in the way of thinking by life itself, in which of course we take an active part.

Is that what you mean when in Fiasco *(and also* Kaddish*) you write: "I was a modestly diligent, if not always impeccably proficient accomplice to the unspoken conspiracy against my life"?*

Precisely. I don't know when it first occurred to me that there had to be a terrible mistake, a diabolical irony, at work in the world order that you experience as part of normal ordinary life, and that terrible mistake is culture itself, the belief system, the language and the concepts that conceal from you that you have long been a well-oiled component of the machinery that has been set up for your own destruction. The secret of survival is collaboration, but to admit that is to bring such shame down on you that you prefer to repudiate rather than accept it. Let's not discuss that right now, however, but the fact remains that when I grasped it, my whole way of looking at things changed. I was able to imagine the language, being, and even frame of thinking of the character in a novel as a fiction, but I was no longer able to become one with him; or rather what I mean to say is that while creating the character, I forgot myself, and for that reason I am unable to give an answer to your original question as to the extent to which the novel character resembles the former me. Plainly, it more closely resembles the person who wrote it than the one who experienced it, and from my own point of view it's very lucky that that is the way it worked out.

Because in this way it released you from nightmarish memories?

Yes, that's right. I was able to slip out of my own skin, as it were, and pull on another one without having to discard the previous one, or in other words, without betraying my experiences.

We shall be jumping a couple of decades ahead, but I feel that this is the place to remind you of an interview you gave in 2003 in which you asserted that you had written Fatelessness *about the Kádár regime, which provoked a huge debate. There were more than a few people who declared that you had betrayed the Holocaust.*

And the debate was just as uninformed and half-baked as the unscrupulous employment of the word "Holocaust."

People don't care to call what actually happened by its proper name—"The Destruction of Europe's Jews," as Raul Hilberg entitled his great work—but instead they have found a word whose true meaning they admittedly don't understand, but they have established this ritual and, by now, ossified and immovable place for it among our notions and they defend it like watch dogs. They bark at anyone who approaches to adjust anything about it. I never called *Fatelessness* a Holocaust novel like others do, because what they call "the Holocaust" cannot be put into a novel. I wrote about a state, and although it's true the novel attempts to shape the unspeakable ordeal of the death camps into a human experience, it was nevertheless concerned primarily with the ethical consequences of *subsistence* and *survival*. That was why I picked the title *Fatelessness*. The ordeal of the death camps becomes a human experience where I come across the universality of the ordeal, and that is fatelessness, that specific aspect of dictatorships, the expropriation, nationalization of one's own fate, turning it into a mass fate, the stripping away of a human being's most human essence. The novel came into being during the Sixties and early Seventies, and what novel does not bear the imprint of its age, its language, its frame of reference, and so on? How could people imagine that the Kádár era was not a dictatorship? It was, the very pick of dictatorships, yet after Auschwitz the virtuality of Auschwitz inheres in every dictatorship. It is only among the obsessions of Hungarian politics that recognizing and admitting this fact could be counted scandalous. In saying that I am not going as far as to assert that the Holocaust was like the Kádár regime; all I have said is that it was

under the Kádár regime that I clearly understood my
Auschwitz ordeals, and I would never have come to understand them if I had grown up in a democracy. And I
have already said that a hundred times, comparing the
strength of memory to Proust's *petites madeleines*, the
unexpected taste of which revived the past for him. For
me the *petite madeleine* was the Kádár era, and it revived
the tastes of Auschwitz.

*If you would permit me to make a comment: you also use
the word "Auschwitz" in an augmented sense, so what is
your objection to the word "Holocaust"?*

It is an instinctive objection. I found the perfect formulation in the book *Remnants of Auschwitz: The Witness and the Archive* by the Italian philosopher Giorgio
Agamben: "The unfortunate term 'holocaust' (usually
with a capital 'H') arises from this unconscious demand to justify a death that is *sine causa*—to give some
meaning back to what seemed incomprehensible." He
also goes into the etymology of the word, the essence
of which is that the original word, the classical Greek
holókau(s)tos, was originally an adjective meaning "totally
burnt"; the history of the word's denotation then leads
into the vocabulary of the Fathers of the early Christian
Church, which we might do well to avoid here. As far as
I'm concerned, I use the word because it has been made
unavoidable, but I take it for what it is: a euphemism, a
cowardly and unimaginative glibness.

*And given its derivation, the word actually only relates to
those who were incinerated: the dead, but not the survivors.*

That's right. The survivor is an exception; his existence—really the result of an industrial accident in the
machinery of death, as Jean Améry so aptly remarked.
Maybe that is one of the reasons it is so hard to accept,
to come to terms with the exceptional and anomalous
existence that survival stands for.

Yet that is not the way you saw it in the concentration camp.
May I remind you of what you said about trust: it was this
trust that helped you in the end to escape.

That's another perspective. Trust existed, but so too did
the interplay of fortuitous circumstances, that even now
I would not dare to dwell upon because it conceals a
dreadful temptation...

The temptation of faith, of providence...

Of explanations—explanations of any sort. I can't remember offhand which author records it, but on his
arrival at Auschwitz he asks an SS guard "Why?" and
the soldier replies "*Hier ist kein warum*—there is no why
here..."

It crops up in Primo Levi's memoir If This Is a Man. *Please*
excuse me, but I need to push you on those whys now all the
same.

I hope that I can't answer your questions, for if I could
that would be as much as to say that I had grasped something that goes beyond the mind's limits. Although, on

the other hand, the mind is there for us to try and use it.

Does that mean to say that I may pose my questions?

Go on, then.

In Galley Boat-Log *you remark that it wasn't easy to fit the sheer fact of survival into* Fatelessness *in such a way that it did not violate the novel's clear and logical composition. In other words, no obstruction of any kind is raised to the linearity of the plot right down to—and I'm using your own ghastly word—the human "debris" in Buchenwald, but the "novelistic" turning point caused you problems. We probably ought to speak some more about that, but would you care to say anything now about how much was fact and how much fiction in that particular series of events?*

Fortunately, I can't answer your question. The series of events conforms to reality. I did lie on a concrete floor, someone did step up to me and cursorily check my reflexes, then take me on his shoulder, and after that everything happened as I describe it. But that in itself already seems beyond the bounds of the credible; even though that is how it happened, I am unable to interpret what happened as reality, only as fiction. The shift from reality to fiction occurred, as I said, when I made a start on the novel. Up till that point the facts—the reality as you would put it—rested mutely within me like a dawn dream that is washed away by the ring of the alarm clock. That reality only becomes problematic if

you analyze it, or in other words if you attempt to bring
it out of the gloom: that is when you immediately realize its impossibility. And by the way, don't think I didn't
try to uncover the *actual* background to that series of
events. I was most curious about the reality that lay behind the *Revier*, or infirmary, with the eiderdown beds;
in other words, how it was possible that in the heart of
Buchenwald concentration camp there could be a hospital in which the patients were able to lie in separate
beds with bedclothes and could receive genuine medical
treatment. In the late 1990s I made the acquaintance of
Dr. Volkhard Knigge, the sterling chap who runs the
Buchenwald memorial. Using my description of the experience as a foothold, all I could say about the room
in which I lay was that it had been called "Saal Sechs,"
or Ward Six. For all our poring over files, facts, and the
material to hand, we were unable to unearth any trace of
such an institution. We did, however, come across one
indirect sign of its existence, for in the roll of Buchenwald prisoners there is a record of an "efflux" to the effect that "Kertész Imre, Hungarian Jewish prisoner No.
64921" died on February 18th, 1945. That was indisput-
able evidence that somebody or several somebodies had
deleted me from the camp roll list to preclude my being
killed as a Jewish prisoner in the event that the camp
were to be liquidated. Anyone who knows even a little
bit about the administrative structure of the concentration camps will know that tacit cooperation on the part
of several people would be required in order to make an
entry like that possible. That trace made me even more
curious, but I had to resign myself to the fact that what

I had experienced exists in my brain alone, in the form of a dreamlike memory. In the winter of 2002, though, while I was in Stockholm, someone telephoned the hotel from Australia—an elderly gentleman by the name of Kucharski, who had been reading this novel by the latest Nobel laureate and in it, to his great excitement, he had come across himself: he had been in the bunk above mine in the *Revier* with the eiderdown beds, and indeed is mentioned by name in the novel. It goes without saying how happy that unexpected call made me; the one drawback being that he spoke only English and Polish, so we had great difficulty in understanding each other, because I don't know a word of Polish and I have only a rudimentary grasp of English. So, the conversation fizzled out somewhere between the two continents, leaving me with the memory of an all-but-transcendental message. Later, Mr. Kucharski's son visited me in Berlin: he has a few snaps taken of himself with me but he was unable to supply any information.

An intriguing story…

Intriguing as intriguing goes; it's just that I could have gone crazy if I couldn't have drawn on it as fiction. As it was, it fitted in superbly with the novel's improbable reality: György Köves can attribute his escape to an incomprehensible absurdity in the same way that the cause of his death would have been an incomprehensible absurdity. An explanation can be found for both cases, but those explanations call for further explanations and so on *ad infinitum*, back to the start of history or the

Creation, if you will. As for *me*, the person who lived through it all yet used the experiences as the raw material for a novel—*I* am able to vanish nicely and comfortably between fiction and the facts that are called reality.

And tread on toward the next novel.

Yes, with the feeling that I may have written a novel but I have solved nothing. The riddle of the world has remained just as tormenting a thorn as it was before.

I know you are reluctant to speak about your camp experiences, but you mentioned just before that the alteration of your record card in Buchenwald would have called for the covert collaboration of several individuals. Who might those individuals have been?

I don't think there's much point in spending much time on the structure of Buchenwald camp. Look, every concentration camp was different from all the others—such was the *"univers concentrationaire."* From a certain point of view (but certainly not mine), Buchenwald in 1944–45 was one of the "less rigorous" camps. That was a result of the ruthless battle that the "red triangle" political prisoners had fought for many years against the "green triangle" criminals. It was a matter of who controlled the internal administration of the camp. The internal administration in its entirety was run by the prisoners, so the ones who had charge of the administration held the power. Since the "red triangle" prisoners were generally more intelligent, more astute, and better organized

than the "greens," they gradually gained control of the
office that handled job allocation and the transports, and
in that way they slowly managed to free themselves of
the criminal elements by channelling them to auxiliary
camps, allocating them to Commandos doing the most
unpleasant work—but maybe it's better I don't go into
the details. As a result, though, the political prisoners
were able to do, and indeed did, quite a lot above all for
the children, for whom otherwise certain death would
have waited in the typhus-ridden barracks of the so-
called Little Camp that was opened for the anonymous
masses of Hungarian Jews in 1944. The long arm of the
politicals probably reached as far as the ramp, where
they tried to fish out and salvage to relative safety a few
lucky devils among the human debris of the transports.

*So there is a rational explanation, after all, for the process
that seemed so irrational to you at the time.*

Even today it seems every bit as irrational, because if I
try to accept the rationality of the whole process that in
the early winter of 1944–45 landed me, half-dead, in an
icy puddle on the concrete of a Buchenwald unloading
bay, there is still no way that I can consider it rational
that I, of all people, and not someone else should have
been rescued from there. If I were to accept that as being rational, I would also have to accept the notion of
providence. But then if providence is rationality, why did
it not extend to the six million others who died there?

Nobody can accuse you of ducking awkward questions, as

*indeed is already very clear from your published work. But
tell me, how can you live facing those questions?*

Like a gambler. I like playing for big stakes, and I am
quite ready to lose it all at any second. As we must all
die, we have the right—even a duty—to think boldly.

*There are quite a lot of people who would say that your way
of thinking is pessimistic.*

I don't know what that means: I wouldn't call dodging
the ultimate questions optimism but plain cowardice.
I can understand it, but an optimist has to die just as
much as a pessimist. Whether we yield to death blindly
or confront it head-on doesn't matter in practice. I would
prefer to confront it head-on because to me that signifies
a fuller life; ultimately it gives me more pleasure. You
could say I am a hedonist.

Not a moralist?

No way! The age of the great moralists—of Montaigne,
La Rochefoucauld, and so on—has long passed. Since
Auschwitz it has become redundant to make any judg-
ments about human nature. The way of the moralist
nowadays leads straight to mass movements, and that is
more than a little problematic, besides which it is boring.
But leave them be: let them believe that there is such a
thing as a just dictatorship without death camps, where
everyone is obliged to be happy. To my way of thinking
happiness means something else—that's all there is to it.

What about justice?

Truth is no longer universal—that's a grave fact, but it must be acknowledged. Standing up for oneself: that's the hardest, it always was. That's precisely what the moralist runs from. Our era does not favour the preservation of the individual; it is simpler to surrender ourselves to salvational ideas than stick to our own unique and irreproducible existence, to choose our own truth rather than *the* truth. But let's not get into this.

Let's carry on with the chronicle. What is your memory of your liberation?

I described it in *Fatelessness*. Those were heady days for us. Every day the order would be given out that Jews were to assemble on the Appellplatz. Death marches set off from the camp to other camps that lay further afield. Every night there was an air raid, and along with the bombs we were able to pick out approaching artillery fire. Over the last few days SS boots thudded on Lager thoroughfares, rifle shots were audible. Finally, around noon one day, the order was bellowed from the loudspeakers that all SS personnel were to leave the camp, "without delay." A few hours later the roar of General Patton's victorious tanks could be heard in the distance. By that night a Hershey bar and a Lucky Strike cigarette had flown onto every bed; in the kitchens the cooks were preparing a thick goulash. We greedily tucked the soup down, but ingesting the heavy food was deadly for more than a few. That was April 11th. The date was murmured at every hand. The loudspeakers, which up till then had relayed the orders of the SS, were switched to the BBC radio broadcasts, which gave news about the liberation of a Buchenwald concentration camp that lay close to the city of Weimar. It was strange to be in Buchenwald listening to the emotional and astonished reports that were made about Buchenwald. It was strange to return of the world of humankind. The rest is just anecdotal.

In Fatelessness György Köves rings the doorbell to the Fleischmanns' home and demands to have his fate given back to him.

That's right. There's no denying that I too rang some doorbell, but I wouldn't swear that my one-time neighbours really were called Fleischmann and Steiner. At the home in Baross Street someone else opened the door: that was the overture to the reality that I had returned to a changed world, but the experience of seeing a stranger at the door instead of my father or stepmother was like a seismic tremor at the time.

Why did you return to Baross Street rather than to Zivatar Street?

When I went away, Baross Street was the status quo, and when I got home I had no way of knowing that my father had died.

True, in the novel that's something you learn from old Fleischmann and Steiner.

Köves learns, though as it happened I too was informed of that by the strangers who were living in the house.

And that important conversation with the two old codgers?

Pure fiction, though it's possible we really did talk about something of the kind. As I have said already, the figure of György Köves more closely resembles the person who wrote the novel than the person who actually lived through it. For the person who wrote the novel the situation was important, the cathartic moment when Köves doesn't just realize but is able to interpret his fate, and in the novel this had to occur in the novelistic time and place that happen to be in the presence of the two old codgers.

I have every respect for your detachment, and the fact that you manifestly prefer to hide behind your novel character rather than tell me what exactly happened to you in those days immediately following your return home to Hungary. Yet as you yourself have already pointed out, the world must have altered profoundly for you.

It is precisely those first days that I have little recollection of; all that's stayed with me are fleeting impressions. When I stepped out of the Western Railway Terminal onto what was then Berlin (later Marx and now Western) Square the sun was dazzling, and a loudspeaker at the stop for the Number 6 tram was blaring out the hit tune "You're the Light in the Night." Next to me there was a fairly well-dressed man who was offering "corn

cakes" from a tray slung round his neck. I remember
the news vendors, or hawkers as they were called, who
would yell out newspaper titles or headlines that one
could never make out. Those first days in general were
ablaze with sunlight; it was summer. I was going around
in a foreign world where I had suddenly caught a whiff
of freedom, especially on the streets. At home people
talked about sombre matters, took stock of their losses
and weighed up the uncertain future that lay ahead. I
couldn't pay much heed to that. I recall the office of the
Budapest-Salgótarján Engineering Works where I took
my mother by surprise. Her female colleagues, whom I
knew myself from the earlier days, all rushed out to hug
me and were deeply moved. The news that I had "come
home from the Lager" spread, and I was asked all manner of stupid questions. I would wake up at night tormented by an unbearable itching. I would switch on the
light, convinced that lice were crawling over me, but they
weren't: my body was covered with red spots, I had an
allergy of some kind. Mother took me to see the works
doctor—a Dr. Bock, as I recollect to this day. He advised
injections of calcium, and I was greatly moved when he
took hold of my arm and carefully inserted the syringe
in my vein: I had grown totally unused to people treat-
ing me that way. In short, I was ringed on all sides by
surprises until everyday life was slowly restored.

How did the news of your father's death take you?

You're asking me an impossible question and forcing me
to resort to banalities.

Perhaps, but I'm still interested.

You may be right. It may be worth considering how my life might have worked out if I had stayed with my father.

Well, how?

Just the same, I suppose, only at the price of yet more grueling fights. Father would obviously have insisted that I take on a "respectable" occupation of some kind, whereas I would have slipped back in a psychosis of permanent rebellion. But if I think about it more carefully, it's possible that I did that anyway, except that I continued my fight against Father without him, which in the absence of his robust presence led to a transcendence. Like an arrow that misses its immediate target and vanishes into the distance.

I beg your pardon, but that's one of Arthur Koestler's similes. Arrow in the Blue *was the title of one of his volumes of autobiography.*

Thank you for reminding me. I've read the book, of course, so my simile may be the product of subconscious Freudian brainwork, but then Koestler, too, was a Jew from Budapest, and he, too, was in conflict with his family, with the bourgeois mode of existence, with Communist salvationism, and ultimately with himself.

As best I know, you, too, became one of Communism's

"*captive minds*," *if I may allude to the title of Czeslaw Mi-
losz's celebrated book.*

Naturally; it would have been a wonder if I hadn't. On
my return from Auschwitz I fell in with an interesting
group of people among whom I soon had to make my
first clear choices: for instance, whether I was to remain
in Hungary or leave, because those were the arguments
that flew around in 1946 and '47 during the "shindigs"
that would evolve out of tea parties into rum drinking
at the homes of those of my classmates who had big-
ger places or at least their own rooms. By then the tidy
order of the B stream had broken down; several of my
Jewish friends had been lost—they perished during the
war or they did not go back to school—or pupils asked
for permission to transfer from the crowded A stream,
or new boys enrolled. The world had changed. One gor-
geous morning in September 1945, when I turned off the
Grand Boulevard into Barcsay Street in order to pick up
my schooling at the Madách Gymnasium where I had
left it before Auschwitz, an edifying scene played out
before my view: gym master Csorba, moustache twitch-
ing, his face terrified, was hurrying toward the Grand
Boulevard with a pack of pupils at his heels, the leader
of whom was yelling with his fist raised in anger: "Lousy
Fascist! The brass neck of you coming back to the school
as a teacher!" That student, incidentally, went on later
to become a well-known film director. We happened to
meet at some reception in the early '90s, and I reminded
him of that long-past scene. He looked at me in amaze-
ment: he had no memory of it.

Really?

I can't say if he really had forgotten, but at all events fifty years later, after another historical turning point—the fall of Communism—he was unwilling to accept that identity. But then again, I think that generation—my own generation—has had to endure too many such wrenching turning points for its identity to remain continuous and intact.

And has your own, I wonder?

There are times when I delude myself into thinking it has, but then at other times I recollect certain periods of my life as though a stranger had lived them, certain actions of mine as if they had not been my actions. But being a writer I am constantly working on my identity, and as soon as I come across it I lose it straight away, because I confer it on the protagonist of one of my novels, so I can start the whole process from the beginning all over again. It's not always easy to be in full possession of ourselves. "Not everyone who is born is in the world," writes Dezső Szomory in that marvellous 1934 novel of his, *Mr. Horeb, the Teacher.*

But you not only were in the world, you also wanted to change the world. You joined the Communist Party...

Not with the aim of seeking salvation for the world, though.

Driven by ressentiment, *perhaps? György Köves comes home from Buchenwald concentration camp, and to the question put to him on the tram by the reporter as to what he was feeling about being back home again and seeing the city he had left, he replies: "Hatred."*

That is one of the most misunderstood, or perhaps better: misinterpreted sentences in *Fatelessness.*

So, let's put it in its proper place.

No, let's not. It's a good thing for a novel to have certain words that live on in readers like a blazing secret.

There are lots of words like that in Fatelessness: *"happiness," for instance, or "homesickness"…*

Words that only gain their full import in their immanence—in the dramatic effect lent to them by place, moment, and the reader's conspiratorial rapport. In a novel certain words can change their ordinary meaning; just as bricks are needed in the construction of a cathedral, but in the end what we marvel at is the steeples and the building that has taken shape through their agency.

So it wasn't salvational zeal that took you into the Communist Party, then, or vengeance.

Much more simple decency, I would say.

Decency? I don't follow.

You might do so better if I were to talk about the necessity of the sense of "belonging somewhere," which people find so self-explanatory. I realized fairly quickly that this need had hoodwinked me and led me into a trap. I tried to believe in something that ran radically counter to my nature and lifestyle; in truth I did not have trouble so much with the object of my "belief"—with Marxism or my "salvational zeal," as you put it—but with "belief" *per se* as a style—I don't know how else to express it. Because it soon became clear that it was useless my trying to close my eyes and explain the world from the viewpoint of a theory of some kind: the truth kept on pushing itself forward and plunging me into unpleasant situations. To begin with I merely found myself at odds with my well-founded doubts, but after the so-called "year of decision" of 1948 the terror set in, and I was astounded to notice that I found myself irredeemably on the wrong side as a result of my own zeal.

Did the realization shock you? Did it change your life?

I don't think so. It was more just a matter of me finding my proper place, if I may put it like that. It put me in touch again with the feeling in which I recognized my life, the feeling that in a certain sense guided me home, and that was a sense of life's absurdity, the simple and inexorable truth of being able to do nothing and being defenceless. In a certain sense it was a completely satisfying feeling that was later to save me from further brooding and posing the wrong questions.

I'm trying to guess what is hidden behind those words. A sixteen-year-old boy who had been in Auschwitz and Buchenwald, goes back to school and prepares to take his school-leaving examinations. Who is still tortured by nightmares...

I wasn't tortured by nightmares. Every now and again it would happen that I was woken by an anxiety that that I had missed *Appell*, the morning muster, but—how to put it?—my "internal clock," that mysterious mental chronometer, was soon reset. I can see from your face that you weren't expecting that. Would you have preferred to hear something a bit more morbid?

I don't appreciate the black humour quite so much on this occasion. I hardly think you would be downplaying the seriousness of experiences you acquired in the death camps quite as much if you hadn't written your works.

But that has given me the right to be totally frank. Look, the fact is that we are having this conversation *now*, and not in 1946 or '47. That is to say, in the meantime I have written my books, and that has obviously altered my memories: they have acquired another character, I might say, maybe even faded, irrespective of the time that has passed. But the fact that I later became a writer in itself presupposes a singular nature. What I have in mind is that more than likely I stand in a different kind of metabolic relationship to reality than do others. What torments most people as an indigestible thought in my case proves all of a sudden to be the raw material for a novel, and as it gains shape I am rid of it. It's not a conscious act, of course; in my younger days it must have been working quite instinctively inside me. As it is now, look-ing back on myself from sixty years later, what I see is a fundamentally cheerful young man, who is greedy for life and will not allow anyone or anything to put him off. Of course, he remembers everything that happened to him, but he fits that into the natural order of things. He doesn't feel any self-pity; he doesn't ask, like so many others, "why me of all people?"; if asked about his expe-riences he talks about them with complete detachment: it's not that he brags about them, but he's kind of proud of them, if you see what I mean. More than that, I'll tell you something even more curious: he calls on their help for the remainder of his life.

Is that what you are referring to in Galley Boat-Log *when you write that the Stalinist dictatorship saved you from feel-ings of major disappointment, indeed from suicide?*[11]

Yes, that's probably so.

There is something that we have not yet clarified. Before you spoke about the sense of belonging, you said that you were carried into Communism by decency. What exactly do you mean?

That one had to take sides. As I mentioned, young people at the time were galvanized by heated debates. The country was in the grip of a great creative zest in the immediate post-war years; at the same time the prevailing conditions were very chaotic. In late 1945 the depreciation in what was then still the unit of Hungarian currency, the pengő, got underway, which over the next six months grew into what is still on record as the greatest hyperinflation in history. Pengő denominations became first "million pengő" then "billion pengő" denominations, with one billion pengős as the basic unit, and even that not for long. Shops would hourly alter the price tickets they displayed. In the spring of 1946, on the terraces of the Budapest cafés such as the "Jeep," the "Liver Fat," the "Moulin Rouge," and the like, customers paid in broken gold for their coffees and whiskeys. The headwaiters carried around tiny scales in their pockets, which they would pull out when the bill was settled and hide away in terror when there was a "raid." An Economic Police force was set up, which not infrequently found itself in pitched gun battles with smugglers and "black marketeers." A person couldn't live from regular wages: factories and offices—including the Budapest-Salgótarján Engineering Works, where my mother worked—paid wages in "kind," giving employees potatoes or flour instead of money. Otherwise, an exultant sense of freedom reigned. A true democracy began to emerge in Hungary for the first time in the country's history, and on the basis of the population's free vote, what's more. But look here! It's not my job to dish out history lessons, but let me mention the alleged testament of the international jurist István Bibó that made the rounds many years later among Budapest intellectuals: "When I die," he is supposed to have said or written, "carve on the headstone of my grave: 'Here rests István Bibó, flourished 1945–1948.'" That says something about the age, wouldn't you agree?

You observed all that from a school desk or the Liver Fat café?

That's a good question. I didn't spend the bulk of my time on the school bench, that's for sure. How could I have? The cinemas were full of viewers for American films, old and new ones alike: Lewis Seiler's *Guadalca-nal Diary*; Billy Wilder's *Five Graves to Cairo* with Erich von Stroheim; Michael Curtiz's *Casablanca*. I devoured war films; I couldn't get enough of the German defeat; it's more than possible that I gave vent to my *ressenti-ment* toward the film screen. Yet I equally enjoyed films like *Broadway Rhythm* with George Gershwin's magical soundtrack—to list them all I wouldn't know where to start. Then again, not far from the school was Pollack's Table Tennis and Billiard Room. We would meet up at eight o'clock in the morning at the school, but by nine or ten o'clock our gang would be either in a cinema or at the ping-pong table, or possibly in the steam bath at the Hungária Hotel. And it was at afternoon teas then that I suddenly discovered girls...

Plus the Communist Party.

Well yes, there must have been some slight connection between the two. Life so had it that I came across mainly girls from well-to-do middle-class families, but I was in the painful position that I never had enough money to pay for them. Our group would engage in vitriolic debates about the meaning of life and the vulgar role played by money: I would win the arguments, but not the girls. I wouldn't be surprised if that was what started my interest in class struggle. But then again, let's face it, society was still full of discredited Fascists. At the time, "Holocaust denial" was as yet an unheard-of concept, of course, but tendencies of that kind had already started to crop up in the press and in private conversations. On the other hand, I was not able to identify with the strictly "Jewish" arguments, either: I was not drawn to Zionism, I was repelled by Jewish self-pity, I had no interest in religion, and I was irritated by a suspicion that I should be seeking out the anti-Semite in everybody. A classless society seemed to me to be truly the best solution, but the very first time I appeared at the "district," I hit the major snag of finding myself face-to-face with a concierge who had been a well-known Fascist in our area. How did he come to be there? Oh yes, he grinned; when the war was over he instantly joined the Party. I had a word with someone—possibly the district Party secretary himself. He then proceeded to explain to me that yes, indeed, Fascism had duped many members of the proletariat, they had to be enlightened—or "re-educated," as he put it—but this was a matter of proletarians who were "capable of progress" and had to be set on the correct path. That rather upset my in any case sensitive stomach, but however averse I was to the concierge and the Party secretary it did nothing to alter my attraction to radical social solutions. After Auschwitz, I felt the correct thing to do was not to base my relationships on personal feelings but on the principles of social progress.

Hmm!

Yes of course! It was bloody stupid of me, as I soon realized.

How did that hang together with all those American films, the billiard hall, the school-leaving exams, and the afternoon teas?

Strange as it may seem, everything did hang together. Something was brewing inside and around me, in my narrower existence and in the wider world. Political dominance, the so-called "year of decision," lay ahead. A sense of being free had never before tapped me on the shoulder, and there, all of a sudden, I was free, albeit not in the best sense, as I had not yet been grabbed by my big, true, lifelong choice. What has been left in me from those three years, as a matter of fact, is an impression of intensive life, but as to whether that was an intellectual experience or rather the volatile vitality of incipient manhood—that I couldn't tell you. Whenever I think of those times I am reminded of Talleyrand's famous utterance: "He who did not live in the years before the revolution cannot know what the sweetness of living is." What I vividly remember is being constantly in love, and I'm not referring to one love in particular (or several) but to my attitude to life itself. Reading a book was for me just as much an erotic experience as peeling a bra from a girl's breasts or losing myself in the melancholy of undistrainable life or the unrivalled sweet happiness with which only the young are acquainted. But I get the feeling that I am starting to lift off into "poetic realms" that in all likelihood are of no interest to you.

How could they fail to be, especially when you talk about them with such relish? And I'm delighted to hear that your life also had such a period when you felt so supremely happy or, to be more accurate, when your life was not being controlled by coercion of one kind or another.

If one disregards the coercion of existing... it did not control my life, admittedly, but it had a strong influence on it.

You were still more or less a student, I suppose, and supported by your mother.

Yes, I was, and that entailed a lot of hassles, above all because I had no pocket money. Differences in our outlooks on life also started to become apparent.

In what respect?

In every respect. We squabbled like a young married couple, except it was not the same of course.

Would you be willing to say more? How did your mother manage to get through the war?

She escaped on two occasions: once from a marching column and the second time from the Óbuda Brick Works, which was a dispatch point for transports to Auschwitz. She told me how it was done, but I no longer exactly recall the details. In the end, she found a "secure" shelter in the Budapest ghetto. After the city was liberated in late

January 1945, she learned that Laci Seres had last been
seen in a death march that had set off toward Vienna:
he had died. Mother was inconsolable, but the residence
in Zivatar Street was still intact: a Hungarian officer
in the Gestapo had picked it in the summer of 1944,
before my mother moved to the "yellow-star house," and
he entered into a regular contract with her—something
to the effect that he was taking over the house for pur-
poses of looking after it, as it were—the sort of arrange-
ment that could only have occurred with my mother,
it goes without saying. As indeed the fact that it was
returned to her in due order, just as it had been, down
to the last coffee spoon, just before the man had to leave
the country in a hurry. Faust made a pact with the Devil,
my mother with a Gestapo officer, and she came off best.
It may be that the Gestapo functionary was a decent
man, as people used to say, though equally he may have
been a mass murderer, but that side of things was of
no concern to my mother. Not that you should think
that was due to moral indifference on her part; no, it
was just that as far as things that did not directly affect
her were concerned she suffered from what was simply
a form of colour-blindness. Not long afterward, an old
friend of hers began to woo her—an engineer, an ex-
pert on vacuum technology, that's as much as I know.
Engineers are fairly dull people as a rule; Uncle Árpád
(that's what he was called) was certainly that unless the
discussion was about vacuums, whereas that was not
exactly the most gripping, from my perspective. My
mother had another admirer as well, a piano dealer. He
was a squat, plethoric, and humorous man; undeniably

he was not as good-looking as the glass-tube engineer, but I always found I could have marvellous talks with him about music. I remember him trying to convince Mother that Bartók wrote extremely melodic music. Entertaining evenings they were. Mr. Kondor, the piano dealer, lived at the other end of town, somewhere in Zugló (the Fourteenth District in Pest). I well remember the freezing-hard winter of 1946–47. Mr. Kondor would come by foot to Buda across the one bridge that functioned at the time, and he would warm his hands up over a coke stove that had been hastily installed on the place of the tile stove. He would offer Mother some corn cakes: Mr. Kondor always brought some delicacy he had purchased on the black market. The talk would quickly turn to music, and I would try to whistle to Mother the main tune of Bartók's Violin Concerto, amid brisk nodding from Mr. Kondor.

So, you were already then interested in music?

It looks like it. I can't recall how I became a regular attender at concerts at the Academy of Music. The fact is I would turn up two or three times a week to see a well-known usher in the main hall.

"That exceedingly testy old man at the Music Academy, known to every student or student type, who, due to some eye defect, wore a perennial look of distrust…"

I can see you are leafing through *The Union Jack*. Carry on, do.

"…but for a forint or two pressed into his palm, [he] would let any student or student type into the auditorium, testily ordering them to stand by the wall and then, as soon as the conductor appeared at the stage door leading to the podium, would direct them in a harsh voice to any unoccupied free seats. It would be fruitless for me to muse now over why, how, and on what impulse I came to like music… it is a fact, therefore, that even then, as little more than a child, I would have been unable to tolerate that life, my life, without music." Is that true?

It is. Later on, when I found myself in situations that made all reality, even my own existence, highly questionable in my own eyes, it was enough for me to softly whistle, let's say, the second subject of the first movement of the Jupiter Symphony for life to be restored to me.

You said that was "later on." When exactly?

When by mistake I set off as a newspaper reporter.

Let's stay for the moment with Mr. Kondor's approval of the young music-lover. We are in the interlude between two dictatorships and you happen to be enjoying the brief interval, or to be posh: intermission.

Not bad.

You're involved in school, in the Communist Party, you go to the Music Academy in the evenings, then sit around in dives by night…

Put like that, it sounds great, and on the whole so it was. Except it leaves out the most important bit, the feeling that most of all dominated my life: uneasiness.

So things weren't entirely all right, after all?

Who said they were? The air rarefied around me; a string of friends, classmates at school, left the country. I felt myself becoming a growing burden to my mother. I hadn't the slightest idea about what I should do by way of setting about my so-called future. For the time being, I still had to take the school-leaving certificate; I used to get up during the night, shut myself into the bathroom, and by the light of the bulb write a universal drama that bore a striking resemblance to the *Divine Comedy*; in my play a man strays from the right path just as in the latter... in a nutshell I think that's what it was about: just as in real life at the time, I lost my way. I had no role models to go by; at grammar school there slowly emerged a sort of elite who spoke in what, to me, was a foreign language. Those boys read Galsworthy and *The Thibaut Family*. With their supercilious intellects, they kept abreast with the mysteries of integral and differential calculus, of which I understood nothing. I acquired the hefty book by Martin du Gard and was bitterly disappointed to have to admit that I found it monumentally boring. What took my fancy, by contrast, were American thrillers, lighthearted Hungarian fiction, like the tales of Jenő Rejtő, Dezső Kosztolányi's "Kornél Esti" short stories, the novellas of Sándor Hunyadi, and Remarque, but if I brought *Arch of Triumph* into a conversation, which I may have read as many as five times, it was to encounter pitying smiles. All in all, I was set to fail the more difficult subjects like math; in the eyes of the elite whom I esteemed so highly I counted as an uncultured clod; sometimes I would find my mother's gaze looking me up and down uneasily and with impatient expectation. I was an exile, yet full of vivid and groundless hopes all the same.

Of what kind?

I don't know—nameless ones. It was as if I had heard the encouragement of a distant promise.

Would that have been the Weltvertrauen, *the trust in the world, that you mentioned earlier as sustaining you in the concentration camp?*

An intriguing question. At all events I lived without any plans, taking each day as it came, but I don't think it is worth dwelling too long on that critical period in my life.

I'm sorry, but crises are always interesting. You yourself just mentioned that you had no role models to go by. Didn't you miss your father, for instance?

The only answer I can give is the brutal one: no, I didn't.

But don't you think that your association with the Communist Party attests to the lack of some kind of father figure?

No, I don't. Right around then I had no connection at all with them. I would pay my Party dues every month; that was the extent of it. In fact, I was assailed by the most severe doubts about Marxism on the basis of a doltishly cocksure book by George Bernard Shaw (I don't recollect its title). I have to start from the fact that among the books belonging to my mother—or Laci Seres, to be precise—I came across a slim, handsome volume with the title of *The Symposium*, written by this ancient Greek author called Plato. I took it to heart for literally days on end. After that came GBS, who solved all of Marxism's problems with a flick of his fly-swatter, simply knocked them on the head, every single one with the same angry swipe. Can one discard everything on which man has been cogitating for five thousand years just like that, I questioned with my eighteen-year-old intellect? That seemed exceedingly unlikely. And then the books on Party tactics by Engels and by Lenin in particular—*One Step Forward, Two Steps Back (The Crisis in Our Party)*, or is it the other way round?—proved mind-numbingly tedious. *The Symposium* was highly refined poetry by comparison.

In other words, you did everything in your power to saw off the branch on which you were perched.

Not *everything*; that only ensued later on. For the time being all I did was make my life more uncomfortable, but that is at least something.

A step ahead?

If I had known which way was backward or forward!

You said just before that you became a newspaper reporter by mistake.

Everything I did was by mistake; all in all, I lived in complete error. Anyway, journalism at least looked interesting.

How did it enter your head to become a journalist?

Look, as I've already said, during the nights I was writing this blank-verse play. Admittedly, I abandoned it fairly quickly, but somehow I had been touched by the process of writing itself. It was around then that Zoltán Jékely's novel based loosely on the life of the poet Endre Ady—*The Black Sail* may have been its title[12]—came into my hands. In this a poet seriously—and quite literally, one might say—seeks death in love, and suddenly there emerges from the perfumed murkiness of a bordello a girl, the bewitching carrier of poisoned kisses, *Hetaera Esmeralda*, as Leverkühn, the main protagonist of a later piece of reading matter, calls the fate insidiously lurking in his blood.[13] As you may be able to tell, I was an incurable romantic whom the world of existing socialism had at one and the same time clutched to its breast. What chance would I have had to get to know myself?

All the same, journalism is rather far removed from romanticism, isn't it?

If you are familiar with it and that's what you do, that's no doubt true, but for me it was the way of life that attracted me, and here too it was through a book: Ernő Szép's novel *Adam's Apple*. A journalist crops up in that who plays the role of the *raissoneur*; wise and resigned, he knows what he knows, he sits in coffee-houses, watching the world bustle by in front of the window table, and every now and again he writes a newspaper article—well, that was exactly how I wanted to live.

I'm not sure your interpretation of the novel is totally accurate...

It doesn't matter: that's how I saw it. Writing as a way of life for me was linked with fatal love, on the one hand, and total idleness, on the other.

Your career in journalism started, as far as I know, with a daily newspaper by the name of Világosság *["Illumination"].*

Yes, it did, and I would find it dreadfully boring if we had to go into the details here.

Fortunately for us you wrote it all down in your novella The Union Jack: *"I was—or ought to have been—pursuing a formulation of life as a journalist," you write. "Granted that for a journalist to demand a formulation of life was a falsehood in its very essence; but then, anyone who lies is* ipso facto *thinking about the truth, and I would only have been able to lie about life if I had been acquainted, at least in part, with its truth, yet I was not acquainted, either in whole or in part, with the truth, this truth, the truth of this life, the life that I too was living." In other words, you were unable either to lie or to tell the truth.*

That's it precisely. I had hit rock bottom. I saw the lies just gushing from the lips of honest people, but I was incapable of doing that, either; to have been able to do so I would have had to withdraw from my existence. Not that that would have been entirely new to me, because in the concentration camp I lived in my dream world; I learned how to be there yet not present. One can do that in any dictatorship.

You said before that journalism at least looked interesting…

It did to start with. That was in the summer of 1948. The country was still ruled by a coalition government, and each of the parties was printing one or two dailies. The various titles would hit the streets from the morning until the late afternoon hours; of course television of any kind did not exist. I was able to breathe the real smell of fresh printer's ink, I would dictate the day's "scoop" over a phone line before we went to press; I was acquainted with a few celebrated chief editors—the last of the Budapest journalists. I lived a pretty exciting life for those few short months. Together with my boss, the editor of the paper's "City Hall" column, we would turn up every morning at City Hall and do the rounds of all the councillors' offices, sniffing around for the latest news. I had a regular accreditation to the City Hall reporters' club.

The doyen of the club was an elderly journalist, Varjas was his name, who worked for the *Kis Újság* ["Small News"], the paper of the Smallholders' Party. In early 1949, the journalists made bets as to whether or not Cardinal Mindszenty would be arrested. I remember word for word what Varjas said: "If they dare arrest Mindszenty, then I say anything can happen here." I met him in the street several months later, and he was in a terrible state. He had forgotten to put in his false teeth that morning; the greying hair that poked out from under a battered deerstalker was matted. His newspaper had been closed down and he had been kicked out. He shook my hand gratefully: "Other people no longer recognize me," he complained.

In The Union Jack *you recount an even more appalling encounter. I'm thinking of the passenger of a black limousine.*

Forget it! That was horrible.

"Before too long I was to be stumbling around in rust-tinted dust beneath the interminable labyrinth of pipes of a murderous factory barrack-complex," you write.

Yes, I was very lucky. In those days dismissal notices were not one of the customary forms of the prevailing relationship between state enterprises and state employees; or at least in the case of intellectuals they generally had other ways of going about it. Firms would preferably fabricate some kind of political conflict, which would often end with the intellectuals being arrested. By contrast, I was handed a regular notice to quit the Szikra Publishing Co.: they would have no further need of my services after January 1st, 1951.

What circumstances did you have to thank for that luck?

My insignificance most likely. Nevertheless, if I was to avoid being liable to prosecution for the criminal offence of "work-shyness constituting a public threat," I had to get a new job within three months. I became a factory worker; there wasn't really any other option.

What was the factory called?

MÁVAG, the Hungarian State Iron and Steel Works.

Ugly name.

No uglier than the factory itself.

All the same, your text seems to glorify the ugliness.

Glorify it? I don't get what you're driving at.

I'll carry on the quotation, if you don't mind: "...bleak dawns smelling of iron castings would await, hazed day-times when the dull cognitions of the mind would swell and burst like heavy bubbles on the tin-grey surface of a steaming, swirling mass of molten metal."

What's your problem with that?

The fact that I gladly read it; more than that, I take a real delight in it. Meanwhile The Union Jack *deals with reality and the aporia of the formulation of reality.*

It doesn't deal *just* with that, but I can begin to see what you're driving at. I won't duck the issue. Like it or not, art always regards life as a celebration.

A carnival, or a memorial service?

A celebration.

But in your case it is precisely the difference that subsists between loathsome material and festal glorification that is so striking.

That's a problem for a moralist, not a writer. Anyone who considers a poet to be a voyeur of horrors and, in a shrill falsetto, forbids him to write poetry after Auschwitz. Is that it?

I am inclined to the view that if one talks about art and dictatorship, one can't avoid Adorno's precept.

"To write poetry after Auschwitz is barbaric." But why are we speaking about this in connection with *The Union Jack*, which doesn't even mention Auschwitz?

Our discussion is not just about The Union Jack *but about your life, which you are continually reformulating. Why? "What experience is for—that's another question, I reflected later... Who sees through us? Living, I reflected, is done as a favour to God," you write.*

Writes the narrator of *The Union Jack,* whom you shouldn't confuse with me, who is putting the words in his mouth. But what has that to do with Adorno?

Just that you insert an otherwordly, metaphysical element between Adorno's sentence and your own sentences, or in plain language, you speak about God where Adorno only sees ignominy.

You know, these are very ticklish matters...

OK, but then let me put it more simply: what is your response to Adorno's famous—or maybe infamous—dictum?

Look here, I learned a lot from Adorno's writings about music, when those were being published in Hungary, but that was all: I never read anything else by him.

You're not answering my question. What is your opinion of Adorno's renowned dictum "To write poetry after Auschwitz is barbaric"?

Well, if I may give a straight answer, I consider that statement to be a moral stink bomb that needlessly pollutes air that is already rank enough as things are.

That's undeniably a straight answer. Would you care to justify it?

I can't imagine how as keen an intellect as Adorno could suppose that art would renounce portraying the greatest trauma of the twentieth century. It's true, though, that the industrialized murder of millions cannot serve as the basis for aesthetic pleasure, as it were, but surely that doesn't mean one ought to regard the poetry of, say, Paul Celan or Miklós Radnóti as barbaric? That's a sick joke, there are no other words for it. And as far as aesthetic "pleasure" goes, did Adorno expect these great poets to write bad poetry? The more you think about that unfortunate pronouncement, the more senseless it becomes. But what I see as truly harmful is the tendency that it reflects: a preposterously misconceived elitism that incidentally runs riot in other forms as well. What I am referring to is the assertion of an exclusive right to suffering, the appropriation, as it were, of the Holocaust. Oddly enough, that tendency concurs with the attitude of the advocates of the "Schlußstrich"—the "finishing touch" stance—the people who would reject having anything to do with the Auschwitz domain of experience and would limit it to a narrow group of people; the people who, with the demise of those who survived the death camps, consider the experience itself as being a dead memory, remote history.

As a Judeo-German conflict that may be regarded as "done and dusted" with the payment of reparations and the erecting of memorials?

In other words, as a purely political issue, although that is not the point. It's precisely what differentiates the

Holocaust (let's stay with that generally accepted label) from all other genocides. I see only one serious problem that needs to be settled, which is whether the twentieth-century experience of concentration camps is a matter of universal or marginal relevance.

We know that you think it is universal, but are you aware that in so doing you are—how should I put it?—stepping out of one cultural area and entering another?

Could you be a bit clearer what you mean?

Universality is a concept from Catholicism.

Oh, I see. A priest once said to me that God has no religion.

You say in Someone Else *that there is no way of getting to grips with Auschwitz unless we take God as our starting point. Let me quote back to you: "If Auschwitz was to no avail, then God has failed; and if God has been made to fail, then we shall never understand Auschwitz."*

Yes, that's the point. Now we shall never understand.

Because God has been made to fail?

Yes, because the world order has not changed even after Auschwitz.

Is that what Liquidation, *your most recent novel, is about?*

Yes. And if in *Fatelessness*—and my other books, too, I hope—I succeeded in turning Auschwitz into a universal human experience, then I must equally report on that failure as a universal human experience. A few critics in Germany did grasp precisely that.

What about here, in Hungary?

Let's just leave it. For Hungary the view on my novel is blocked by the towers of Stockholm. I don't wish to say any more than that.

I find that hard to believe, but we'll come back to this later. What is of interest to me right now is how you managed to shake off the factory.

Through an act of humiliating solidarity of the kind that sometimes appears almost as a memento at critical turning points of my life.

Why do you say "humiliating"?

Because they are unmerited when they occur to me, and they leave me defenceless. I am always embarrassed when the world order is infringed.

What would you call the world order?

The banal spell of evil.

This is beginning to interest me. Let me repeat my question: How did you manage to get out of the factory?

One afternoon, the foreman said that a journalist was waiting for me outside, in the changing room. To be brief, it was Nándi Ordas, who was working on what was called the "Manufacturing" column for my old newspaper (which had long ceased to be called *Világosság* but was named *Evening Budapest* instead, on the lines of some Soviet model). He was a young chap from the provinces, twenty-five or thirty years old, burly and fresh-faced, though he was fonder of a spritzer or two more than was good for him. We had hit it off from the start but more from a distance, simply not having enough time to become real friends. As "Manufacturing" reporter he had access to any factory and even some of the ministries. "I've wangled this job for you," he said in elation as I entered the changing room.

Had you asked him to sniff around?

Not at all! I wasn't even sure whether he had noticed I had been kicked out. I hadn't had time even to say farewell. "Just go along to the Ministry for the Metallurgical and Engineering Industries and ask to see the head of the press office, Márton Fazekas. He already knows everything." That's how it was. Next morning I was seen by a gentleman (or rather "Comrade") of around fifty, wiry, on the short side, a very soft-spoken chap wearing a snazzy sports jacket, a hint of melancholy on his well-groomed moustachioed features...

A flower adorning the buttonhole of his jacket...

How do you know that?

I've read Fiasco.

Oh yes, right you are. But the figure you meet there is not the real Márton Fazekas but a semistylized, I might almost say mythical mutant of him. True, the real Marci Fazekas also wrote poetry that, every now and again, he would read to me in confidence, under a huge map of Korea that hung on his office wall.

What has that to do with the poems?

What do you mean?

The map of Korea...

In those days there was a map of Korea pinned up in every office, workroom, and workshop in the country, everywhere. There would be pins with red flags to track the victorious advance of the North Korean forces: the pins would have to be reset every day in accordance with the military situation, accompanied wherever possible with a picture or article cut out of one paper or another that showed the South Korean army in full retreat and/or General MacArthur and his threats to launch an atomic bomb attack.

Yes, of course, the Korean War.

You weren't even born when that was in progress. To be brief, we lived in an intoxicating succession of unbroken Korean victories until, all of a sudden, with the invasion and battle of Inchon, the maps of Korea were removed from the walls overnight. We then started to send missives to the American president (whether it was Harry Truman or Eisenhower, I don't rightly recall). "Dear Mr. President," the letters proclaimed, "We, employees of the Press Office of the Ministry for the Metallurgical and Engineering Industries, demand the immediate termination of American involvement," and so on, with the letters all signing off "Hands off Korea!"

Madness!

Yet there was method in it, as Hamlet says.

Which prompts me to note that we are flitting about fairly erratically. So, Márton Fazekas took you on as a colleague at the ministry. When was that exactly?

In the early spring of 1951.

What were your duties, strictly speaking?

If only I had known... the biggest trouble, though, was that I couldn't care. In principle, I should have been putting together pieces along the lines of a newspaper article, but I had already been kicked out of the newspaper because I was incapable of writing material like that.

Yet all the same, Fazekas didn't kick you out.

His bad luck was that he had taken a liking to me. He

soon realized, however, that I was only using the job as a cover against the hostile world outside, but he looked on me as a sort of "young talent" who needed to be supported.

Did you mention your literary ambitions to him?

It could be... At the time I, too, was giving the co-authorship mode of existence a trial. You're no doubt familiar with Iván Mándy's scintillating book, *Lecturers and Co-authors.*

You bet! Did you use to go to his regular haunt, the "Darling" café?

No, I used to frequent the espressos along Andrássy... oops! Stalin Avenue, the former "Broadway" of Budapest. You know, ten or twenty years ago I was able to spout one anecdote after another about that period, which the now legendary Pál Királyhegyi probably got nearest to nailing: "One of these days, I'm going to write the story of my life under the title *My Happy Days of Being Bored to Tears by Terror,*" as he was in the habit of saying. The pristine flavour of those ridiculous and yet horrific times has been lost.

Fortunately, you managed to retrieve some of that in the extraordinary menagerie of your novel Fiasco. *But let's get back to Fazekas...*

In point of fact, Fazekas was a very civil fellow; he

mildly chided me on a few occasions, but in his own mind he rationalized what was, at root, a paternal sense of responsibility towards me which, in some way or other, involved literature and an unspoken Jewish solidarity.

Did you ever talk about that?

I think Fazekas was aware that I had passed through Auschwitz.

That was it?

It was something that never came up openly in conversation between us. If he did know, it could only have been from my so-called "cadre," or Party-worker, record card—the secret document that followed one around, like an invisible shadow, from office to office.

I would really like to push you further about that, but I have to confess that the subject makes me, as a non-Jew, rather uneasy.

One of those "tricky topics," right?

Sadly, that's still the case in Hungary. I don't know if it's a question that it is in any way legitimate to pose…

Pose it, then I can either choose to reply or not.

I would like to ask you about that Jewish solidarity.

Obviously, in a dictatorship that cannot have operated overtly; what I mean is that no one was able to define himself as a Jew...

Unless you went to the rabbinical training school, and provided the regime did not define you as a Jew, as was the case two years later, when the trial of those accused of involvement in the Jewish doctors' plot got underway in the Soviet Union.

I understand. But did you, for instance, instantly identify Fazekas as being Jewish?

That's a good question. In all probability: yes, but not in a conscious fashion. In other words, I wouldn't have said to myself that this fellow Fazekas is Jewish, but I would have sensed that I could have a certain degree of trust in him.

Because he was Jewish.

Because we had similar... it would be hard to say what. Not faces or ways of thinking... I think that the only thing two Jews have in common is their fears; that's how they can be distinguished most accurately, at least in Central and Eastern Europe.

That seems to run counter to the fact that Rákosi, Gerő, Farkas, in short virtually the entire Stalinist leadership in Hungary at that time, were themselves of Jewish extraction. Is that something you have thought about?

No. I was aware of the fact, of course, but it's not something that preoccupied me in any way at all. Did the fact that Szálasi and the entire leadership of the Arrow-Cross Party in Nazi Hungary were Christians give you any pause for thought?

Touché.

Look, the most destructive passion of the twentieth century was the relinquishment of the individual and the levelling of collective accusations against whole populations and ethnic groups. If we are going to start analyzing the degree to which I, as a Jew, bear responsibility for the deeds of a total stranger purely on the grounds that he, too, was born Jewish, then that is tantamount to accepting that way of thinking and crossing into the realm of ideology. Only in that case, I don't know what we would have to talk about; I feel I am doing far too much explaining as things are.

I agree, but all the same, people do have various prejudices, out of which it is possible to forge political capital.

Undeniably, but the understanding the two of us had was not that we were going to talk about the sick aberrations of politics.

I won't push it any further, because I made it clear from the start that I wanted to broach a touchy subject. I hope that you don't take it amiss and I can count on your continued assistance.

Now we have started, I'm not going to leave you in the lurch.

In that case, let's resume with fear. You said that the most two Jews have in common is their fears. To what extent did fear shape you?

I wasn't afraid. To that extent, Auschwitz truly was a great school. What made me Jewish was the Holocaust, and that is a new phenomenon in Europe. Of course, I would not have been able to formulate it as clearly as that at the time. But later on I set myself a task in life that required me to clarify for myself the quality of my Jewishness, if I may put it like that. For instance, I would have a hard job discussing Jewish metaphysics, Jewish culture, or Jewish literature with you because I am not acquainted with these things. In that sense I am not Jewish at all. Yet that is of no interest to anyone the moment I am taken off to Auschwitz, or made the main defendant in a show trial. Then you are struggling for sheer survival and are no longer able to say that you believe you are not Jewish…

What are you, according to your conviction?

Jewish—but a Jew who has nothing in common with any of the Jewish modes of life that were known before Auschwitz, neither archaic Jews, nor assimilated Jews, nor Zionist Jews. Or with Israel. That may be the hardest thing of all to say.

It took you half a century. In 2002 you wrote a travel diary to which you gave the title "Jerusalem, Jerusalem."[14] Nevertheless, let us stay for a bit longer on the time you spent with Fazekas. By then it was six years since you had got out of Buchenwald, you're twenty-two; so, back then, in 1951, what did a Jewish identity mean to you?

Anecdotes, Jewish jokes, a certain protection with Fazekas—in other words, nothing, nothing at all, so I think there is little sense in using the term "identity" here. I didn't have an identity, and I didn't miss having one, either.

You already stated that when you were talking about your childhood.

In a certain sense I was still living my childhood then as well. Dictatorships make children out of people inasmuch as they do not permit existential choices and thereby deprive one of that wonderful burden of being responsible for oneself. At that time I lived in a fantasy world that was impossible to keep any check on, perfectly absurd; I was concealed in my insignificance.

The words ring a bell; they're from Fiasco, *aren't they, but what do they mean, more precisely?*

Total vulnerability to chance. I compared myself to a person who is cast this way by chance, like a light skiff by a swift current. Whereas I just gave in to physical appearances and considered myself to be a singularly nebulous person, whom I did not know at all and thus who served as a constant source of surprises.

It must have been a strange state.

Parlous in the extreme.

Is that how you judge it now, or did you perceive it as dangerous at the time?

I don't know. The drawback of conversations like this is precisely the fact that one speaks self-confidently about one's life in the sure knowledge of where it has ended up, but are you able to conjure up the person you were, your aimlessness? Can you feel under your feet the tightrope that you danced on? Did you even know that you were dancing on a tightrope? Years later, I came across that immortal adage from Duchamp: "There is no solution, because there is no problem." Probably one has to evoke trivial details, though often even that proves futile. Not long ago, for instance, I mulled at length over what I ate in those days. What did I eat during a period when practically all items of food were only sold in exchange for ration coupons? Who washed my underwear, and how? I recollect that there used to be one of those posh, old-fashioned public lavatories in front of the EMKE café, on the corner of the Grand Boulevard and Rákóczi Avenue. There were steps that led down to it. A decrepit crone who was a leftover from the *"ancien regime"* was in charge of it as the WC attendant. One even got a bar of soap from her, which had to be given back after one had washed. Other than that, I used to go to the Lukács Baths to wash down and have a swim—I remember that well. There were times when I was only able to get to the swimming baths in the evening, when the green waters of the pool would be lit up by searchlights a bit like spotlights. Those years dropped out of my life like loose change through a hole in a purse; it would be useless to try to gather them together now. On a sunny but gusty winter morning not long ago, I took a walk through the Városmajor Park in Buda and cut over the tramlines to reach Logodi Street[15] in order to look for the house where I had been a subtenant what is now a good fifty years ago. I have long since forgotten the house number, so I tried to recognize it from memory: it just didn't work. I traipsed back home. I began to realize that I shall never again make sense of my young days: I don't know what I did, and why, how and why I became the person I became.

For my part, though, I hope we shall learn something about this in the end. You mentioned Logodi Street, which suggests that you were no longer living with your mother in Zivatar Street.

No, my mother married the glass engineer, who had in the meanwhile been promoted to managing director of the factory.

For political reasons or engineering know-how?

I suppose it was as a reward for all his inventions; he

wasn't interested in anything besides vacuum tubes. My mother, on the other hand, was finally able to live in the style she had dreamed about since her girlhood. There was a car that went with the position, and at weekends they would go off on shoots for game, have a pig slaughtered in autumn for the hams and sausages... and as a result of some property deal they swapped the Zivatar Street apartment over my head.

Effectively, put you out on the street?

Only in principle; in practice they arranged a subtenancy for me "on a friendly basis" as the main tenant was some sort of senior employee at the factory that my stepfather managed.

In other words, more through bribery than "on a friendly basis"...

That's quite possible, as we settled on a ridiculously low rent; but the main thing was that it was a rather neat room at the foot of Buda Castle Hill, with my window overlooking the dense leafage of a tree. Since this meant we were finally free of each other, the endless wrangles with my mother also grew less common.

What were the wrangles about?

Look, I've already told you that in matters of no direct concern to her my mother suffered from outright colour-blindness. Both she and her husband pretended that we were living in a slightly wacky but otherwise completely normal world, in which a young person's duty is to attend to their advancement and build a career. This was the summer of 1951. Every night, toward dawn, operatives of the State Security Office, the ÁVH, would go around the city loading onto trucks and transporting to their forced places of residence those people who had been sentenced to resettlement.

You mentioned earlier Iván Mándy's book, Lecturers and Co-authors...

Yes, and that too was part of the total absurdity. At that time I was part of a small group of friends who would write humorous sketches and short radio plays, all kinds of nonsense, for the insatiable Hungarian Radio. We would take apart the elements of the plays of Ferenc Molnár in various dives and espresso cafés, quite convinced that we would soon become famous comedy writers.

In Fiasco *there is a scene where Köves, getting on for daybreak, is making his way homeward along deserted streets and is hailed by a strange chap from a bench by the footpath...*

The pianist, who didn't dare go home, because he wanted to avoid being dragged away from his bed.

Is the pianist a figure you dreamed up, or is he someone you encountered in real life?

I could even tell you his name.

That scene, as it happened, you also wrote as a stand-alone short story under the title "The Bench," which contains a very typical sentence about the nonexistent identity that you spoke of before. It runs: "In those days I could always be persuaded by anything if I came up against the necessary patience or robustness."

That is probably how it was in fact.

I rather feared as much. What, then, did it take for you to come to your senses from this, as it were, semidetached state?

Maybe by first getting fully immersed in it, then, later on, simply recalling it and being duly astonished by it.

As if by means of a time machine, you were to arrive at an unfamiliar—or perhaps familiar—place and uneasily watch what is happening to you?

If you're referring to the second part of *Fiasco*, then you're on the wrong track. Köves knows exactly what is going to happen to him; indeed, he himself provokes the events.

He is tormented by a Kafkaesque guilty conscience and forebodings.

Not at all. I know that an interpretation along those lines was printed in a German newspaper...

*Which claims that you are trying to amplify on Kafka, rais-
ing the question of whether that is in fact possible.*

That's not the point; the real issue is whether it is possible, in certain circumstances, not to amplify on Kafka.
And here I don't mean Kafka's incomparable genius,
but the fact that history has vindicated Kafka, and that
has left its mark on the literature of succeeding genera-
tions. The language of the second part of *Fiasco* caused
me quite a headache, i.e., how it is possible to cast the
ephemeral ideological constructs of merely transitory
closed regimes and dictatorships into the more durable
form of a novel. I was looking for a usable metaphor, and
it finally occurred to me that totalitarian dictatorships,
including the Stalinist one, speak in the language of religion. Nor can it be otherwise, since their world was
not a realm of logic but of the absurd. As a result, therefore, a degree of Kafkaesque stylization seemed glar-
ingly obvious, for one thing because *Fiasco* ultimately
deals with something entirely different from Kafka's
marvellous novels; for another thing, because what else
is the intellectual domain that we call literature other
than the handshaking of writers with one another *ad
infinitum?* But that would take it too far. As far as *Fiasco* is concerned, it is a novel based on a fundamentally
amusing notion. A writer bogged down in the intellectual swamp of the Seventies, the Brezhnev era, awakes
to the realization that he is working counter to his own
interest, because a creative life cannot be squared with
the time in which he is living. That is when he embarks
on a novel, which is nothing more than a process of the

recapitulation of a fate: episode by episode, he recreates the existence of his young *alter ego*, Köves, looking more and more for where he lost his way, why he couldn't disappear, submerge, into the anonymous mass of history. He is unlucky, however, and at the end of the book comes to the very same point—the L-shaped corridor— where he was once overtaken by his creative vision: the creative life proves to be an inescapable curse, its end product failure—the fiasco.

It may well be that I am lacking something in the humour department when it comes to this, but I can now clearly see that the plot of the novel-in-the-novel which is "Fiasco" is not in the least the dream parable that it is usually interpreted as being.

I could only give a response if I knew what, precisely, you think of as a "parable." Can you give an example?

Offhand, Orwell's Nineteen Eighty-Four *comes to mind as being a true parable.*

In that case, *Fiasco* cannot be one. It contains a different ratio of fiction and real life. Or rather, if one wants to see it as a parable, then it's not a very good one. But there are other genres that *Fiasco* also does not belong to. To be brief and parabolic myself: it is not appropriate to use a nutcracker to peel a peach.

Witticisms aside, obviously what you want to say is that

the novel should be approached from the point of view of its own originality.

Everything should be approached from the point of view of its own originality.

Despite the fact that it is no simple task to get to grips with Fiasco: it is surrounded by as many defensive systems as a fortification. The moment you have managed to struggle past one you find yourself face-to-face with another. You have to fight your way past one parenthesized barbed-wire fence after another, past ever newer crevasses of novels-within-novels... until it finally dawns on you that that is exactly what the novel is about: intellectual brackets and mental barbed-wire entanglements. Am I assessing that correctly?

The subject of the novel is enclosure, that's for sure, and that has formal consequences. In essence, it's a matter of a musical structure that is followed as a structural principle.

You assign a big part to music in the construction, or I should say the composition, of your novels.

I don't think that can be of interest to anyone except myself, but it's true that I like to conceive of my novels in terms of a musical composition.

In other words, it's not just a matter of the musicality of individual sentences...

No, of the whole, of the complete composition. With *Fiasco*, for instance, the beginning and end of the novel overlap, but this is achieved with musical tools: the images of the "enlightenment" and the L-shaped corridor are snapped twice by the text, then the third time they come true... but those are just my own distinctly dubious private amusements and can only be boring to readers.

Not to me, that's for sure, because I would like to find my bearings in what is perhaps the most enigmatic of your novels. With Fatelessness *you employed a simple linear technique...*

That was not exactly simple, either, but in that instance the linear technique expressed some important ideas. With *Fiasco*, on the other hand, I made a deliberate effort to "transcribe" the time-planes onto one another, and, just like music, the novel, too, unfolds over time, and in that way a circular novel structure came into being.

A circle that encloses within itself both the Nazi concentration camp and the Communist jails.

Yes, in the end I wanted to pluck out the *danse macabre* of the two regimes on a single string, despite the fact that I wrote and published *Fiasco* before the change in regime and therefore when censorship was still very much in force.

Toward the end of Fiasco, *Köves sends a letter to Berg, who is one of the most mysterious of all the novel's figures, in which he relates his strange experiences. In addition, this is where Köves, for the first and only time in the novel, speaks in the first person singular, which lends an air of confessional authenticity to the text...*

So, we're again mooring by the unfathomable relationship between fiction and reality, yet we already covered that at the very start of our conversation. Only now I get the impression that you are not quite so sure of yourself as you were then.

Well, I'm frightened that you are going to tell the truth...

Never doubt it!

All right, then, let's start off from the previous chapter of "Fiasco", *the novel-in-the-novel, where we learn that Köves has been in the army "because the same post as the dismissal letter from the ministry had also brought a demand that he immediately discharge his deferred military service." When did that happen in your case?*

In November 1951 I was called up for regular military service, and after the three months of so-called "basic training" it turned out that the military command had singular plans for the unit to which I had been posted...

"Yet what a filthy dream did I wake up to all at once! I

*am standing in a room by a desk behind which is seated an
obese, hormonally challenged bonehead, with matted hair,
rotting teeth, bags under his eyes, and a sneer on his face: a
major, and what he wants is for me to put my signature at
the bottom of a piece of paper and accept a post as a prison
guard in the central military prison." What that sounds like
is that Köves, on the model of many other literary figures, is
about to enter a contract with the Devil...*

It's not a huge difference in principle.

*If I look on it as a literary game. But here, as it is said in one
of Wedekind's plays, "we're not playing but living." So, why
does Köves sign the paper?*

Out of ignorance, curiosity, and, above all, existential
apathy.

*"...my existence went to sleep, or was paralyzed inside me,
or at any rate it gave no twinge of unease to warn me of the
importance of the decision," writes Köves, or is that you?*

I write "the Old Boy" who writes Köves, who in turn
writes the letter addressed to Berg.

*"That was when I raised my hand and struck a defenceless
prisoner in the face"—who writes that?*

Köves.

And Köves is who, exactly?

You can't be serious. "I am Madame Bovary"—for any lesser risk it's better if one doesn't sit down to write a novel.

It seems that I'm not only lacking something in the humour department but in the horror department as well. I don't know you to be the sort of person who would strike somebody in the face.

You can't know, just as Köves does not know himself: we spoke about that earlier on when we talked about him being concealed in his insignificance. Here you, the reader, step with Köves into a world where the aimlessly stumbling personality has no foothold, and if your "existence has gone to sleep," it is easy to make—or let's say rather: it can easily *happen*—the first and decisive step, from which there is no turning back.

If one accepts that argument, then it would be impossible to call any mass murderer to account.

You are forgetting that as a writer I am not concerned with calling people to account but with accurate portrayal. In any case, I—and the "I" here is an unknown factor, a passivity—so, I was lucky and I was not exposed to any haunting moment like that.

Do you really think it is just a matter of luck?

I don't know. On the basis of the experiences I gained in camps and dictatorships, the resilience of human nature is inexhaustible. When I wrote that novel—almost thirty years after the fact—I certainly had to ponder the possibility of such a moment. In the last analysis, the imagination is also a kind of reality, and if I really wished to respond to the issues raised in the novel, then I had to carry out in my imagination things that had not happened in reality if only in order that the fictional Köves should experience the "definitive act" and place it at Berg's disposal.

Before we began this conversation, I sat down to re-read "I, the Executioner," the novel-in-the-novel-in-the-novel of Fiasco, *which provides an apology for mass murder. Do I understand correctly that the state when a person is freed from his own personality and completely subsumes it to the executioner's role is one that Berg calls grace?*

Or that of the victim. "It might perhaps be pleasant to be alternately victim and executioner," Baudelaire remarks in *My Heart Laid Bare* on the basis of who knows what earlier experiences he may have had. The essence of both roles is a complete release from the burden of personality—that is why Berg is searching for a "definitive act" that would set the executioner on the "salvational" route of mass murder.

What do you mean here by a "definitive act"?

It's an act which does not ensue from the propensities, character, or individuality of the person concerned but solely from the situation, which commands the terrain like a foreign power. The moment takes command, and you get out of it as best you can. You have to free yourself of the colossal tension: all of a sudden, you cave in and abandon any resistance—relinquish yourself to the line of least resistance, one could say.

Is this not the same thing as what elsewhere you refer to as fatelessness?

In essence the same thing; it's just that the idiom employed in *Fiasco* is different.

There it is referred to as "grace," and it is given a positive connotation. Why is that?

Because in Berg's view, man has become superfluous in a dictatorship. The only way he can find the grace is by what he refers to as "service," "serving the order."

In the form of either villain or victim... If we did not have the written records that were left behind by the various dictatorships, I would venture to say that we would have no idea what this man was talking about. Even as things are, his figure is fairly shrouded in mist. Who exactly is he?

I suppose that in Berg's figure I was constructing an imaginary representation of the "Old Boy" whom one gets to know in the frame novel. He's a man of absolute theory, who is pondering "a plan for a dissertation, on a not-too-ambitious scale, concerning the possibilities for an aesthetic mediation of violence."

In other words, the figure of the "Old Boy" is replicated, as it were, in the Köves novel?

Precisely—rather like a cinema film shot through a prismatic lens. The scenes with Köves and Berg, followed by Köves's epistolary confession, are the culmination of the novel, the place where the entire burden of argument is brought to a terse climactic point around them.

One in which Berg goes mad, whereas Köves carries on and then suddenly finds himself in the L-shaped corridor... which is where he is overtaken by a moment of rapture.

Of enlightenment.

My apologies for the loose language. In any event it is a matter of a mystical moment, an experience that one cannot recount in the language of rationality but which, one could say, abruptly changes one's life. What in fact did happen to you in the corridor?

I have already said this several times, and I fear that I shall be guilty of repeating myself. Or rather I fear that I won't be able to put it like... like for example...

Like you put it in Stockholm.

Stockholm is several light years away from the place where we are holding this conversation. And it may well be that our path does not lead to Stockholm, anyway.

What do you mean by that?

That we have yielded to this flawed logic several times already. We are sitting here at total ease and safety at the endpoint of our story and contentedly chomping away about the splendid triumphal procession. We are divesting ourselves of any risk, because every step we take is another step toward the goal, and we can have complete confidence in each and every step: everything we do is correct, because we are progressing towards our goal. That is why we boarded the train that chuffed toward Auschwitz; that is why I was not shoved to the left by the doctor at the Birkenau selection; that is why kindly hands hauled me out from among the corpses at Buchenwald, and so on… in that way the story would come to pass, except it would not be a Job's story of making atonement, as you might suppose, but of a vulgar kitsch, the career of a ridiculous buffoon. Every individual story is kitsch, because it evades the rules; every single survivor attests purely to a breakdown in the machinery that has occurred in an individual case. Truth belongs only to the dead, no one else.

But the dead keep their counsel… the truth belongs to those who speak out. You yourself said that; I read it somewhere in Galley Boat-Log.[16] *Let me put rather the following question: What was the immediate outcome, or consequence if you prefer, of the enlightenment you underwent in the L-shaped corridor?*

That for weeks or months on end, or however long it was, I wrote and wrote a text that drove me to despair every day, because in no way would it assume any shape, coalesce into an organic whole. It bubbled out from somewhere deep inside me like scalding-hot lava and then spread out amorphously, destroying everything around.

That sounds pretty alarming—rather as though you were recounting being possessed by a deleterious passion.

Precisely. Every day I would write something that, when I read it over at the end of the day, I would find dispiriting. The next day, despite my ever-growing sense of dismay, I would nevertheless start all over again...

What caused that "ever-growing sense of dismay"?

The fact that I had to give way to the demands of the text. I had to recognize that the sentences that would appear under my hand would sometimes arrive unexpectedly: they knew more than I myself did; they would surprise me with secrets that I was unaware of; they would not tolerate my interventions but lived some sort of autonomous, alien life that it was up to me to understand rather than dominate... slowly the threatening thought dawned on me that I needed time, more time, in fact a great deal more time...

In order to prepare for your career?

The word "career" is totally out of place here. My so-called career is at best the product of a construct in hindsight—that's if anyone should seek to slip in the fallacy of logic into processes that are otherwise spontaneous and inexplicable. Forget the career and try instead to imagine a completely bewildered young man who, not knowing why, started to write, sharpened pencils, and spread sheets of blank paper in front of himself while noting with horror that there was nothing to justify his actions—indeed, what he was doing was frankly nonsensical.

Despite that, every day you carried on with your apparently senseless experiments. Why?

Out of an existential angst that may have silenced everything else inside me.

Existential angst... could you label that any other way?

A compulsive psychosis... categorical inner imperative... the fulfilment of a task... how should I know?

Not a bad task. Did a sense of vocation awaken in you, perhaps?

No way! I have many faults, but I never felt a sense of vocation.

Maybe that was the way in which your talent manifested itself.

Yes, talent is one of those words that is used, but no one knows what it means.

"In the end it may yet transpire that I do, indeed, have some talent for writing, which would make me truly sorry," writes the Old Boy in Fiasco, *"since I did not start writing because I have talent; on the contrary, when I decided that I would write a novel, evidently I also decided, by the bye, that I would become talented. I needed it; there was a job to be done. I had to aim to write a good book, not out of vanity but in the nature of the thing, so to say."*

Well, yes, but at that point in time, at rock bottom, I couldn't have known that I was going to be so wise thirty years later.

If you didn't realize it, you have still not answered my earlier question as to what, in fact, happened to you in the L-shaped corridor.

Let's just accept that not every question has an answer.

"There comes a moment in the lives of men when they suddenly become aware of themselves and their powers are freed; from this moment onward we can reckon to be ourselves, this is the moment when we were born," you write in Galley Boat-Log.[17]

One can hardly go further than that. I recollect an ecstatic moment that I could only capture here and now with rather vacuous words.

All the same, that was the moment that determined the further course of your life.

That is undeniable.

Which forced you to the writing desk, which held you prisoner among your papers—is that what you call "existential angst"? What sort of text was it that you were in fact struggling with? Was it a novel, a short story, a diary, memoir?

Let me put it this way: a longish short story.

One that, as you said, refused to assume any shape. What happened to it in the end? Did you discard it?

Fortunately, no. The better passages from it found their way, thirty years later, into the novel-in-the-novel of *Fiasco.*

With appropriate alterations, no doubt.

Without changing a word.

Surely you don't mean the novel that Berg reads out to Köves under the title "I, the Executioner"?

Yes, I do.

Staggering authorial economy! And incidentally, it does not show the least trace of thirty years of dust. However, I do now begin to see how you worked out the path that would lead you to Fatelessness.

I'd quite like to know myself.

You sought atonement for what you lived through in prison, only in doing so you amplified your problem into one of global dimensions. The only possible solution was a novel— in your case, at least, since you were born a writer.

I don't know; one is not born for anything in particular, but if one manages to stay alive long enough, then one cannot avoid eventually becoming something... and incidentally what you refer to as the path to *Fatelessness* I experienced as a continuous deficiency, and the fact that I gave myself to writing *Fatelessness* I intended as a fulfilment of that disaster, as a kind of self-punishment. Because I found I was just getting nowhere with fiction writing. "At least you are familiar with the material," I told myself with a degree of healthy scorn, planning to write it in a couple of months.

When was that?

In 1960.

And the couple of months became thirteen years, if I'm not mistaken. But that is to depart from the chronological sequence... when did the incident in the L-shaped corridor take place?

Precisely when, I couldn't tell you myself. I'd put it somewhere around... late 1955. I recall it was autumn and it was raining. By then I was trying to get by as a "freelance"—a form of life that did, indeed, lead to some rather tight spots at times when it came to making a living. Anyway, around then one or two of my friends were working for the *Magyar Nemzet* [Hungarian Nation] newspaper, and the editor of one column or other asked me to write a piece on why the trains were running late. As a result I found myself in an L-shaped corridor in one of the Hungarian State Railway offices—somewhere near the Eastern Railway Terminal, I seem to recollect.

Hang on a moment! The last time we had a glimpse of you was in uniform, as an army conscript. First of all, you had to be discharged... as far as I know, you got involved in a fairly risky venture to that end.

You could call it that. But it's anecdotal, so let's keep it as short as possible.

You fainted in public at one of the morning parades, didn't you?

Yes, I did. Beforehand, I had borrowed several medical texts from the library to study, above all, the various species of neurosis with particular regard to fits and the catatonic state. I collapsed and went into a crying fit, which was followed by muscle rigidity and so on. The main thing was to remain consistent.

As best I know, you were even admitted to the hospital.

I'll spare you the details. The doctors didn't know what to make of me.

"After all, everything depends on the firmness of our will, and in my experience a person can cross over into madness with terrifying ease, if he wants that at all costs," Köves writes in Fiasco.[18]

That's right.

When did all this happen?

In the summer and autumn of 1953.

If what you say in your book Someone Else *is accurate, you became acquainted with your first wife, Albina, that same autumn.*

Yes.

The story goes that the long hot summer of that year was followed by a mild autumn.

That's how it was.

One fine evening in September you were strolling lazily down Andrássy (then Stalin) Avenue towards Nagymező Street, dropping in on the cafés that were on your way. In what was then nicknamed the "Sissi"[18] bar at the Moulin

Rouge there was just one couple sitting in the semi-gloom into which it was plunged by the burgundy plush of the stools and the dark purple of the wall hangings: a tow-haired, broad-shouldered water polo player with whom you had a fleeting acquaintance and a strange woman. They invited you to join them at their table.

Yes.

The woman was not pretty to your way of thinking, but very alluring. Her quirky humour struck you immediately. What was it she asked?

"Can a person doss at your place?"

"*Doss*"?

Stay, get a bed, in the slang of those days.

You were somewhat surprised at the unforeseen familiarity, but you instantly replied that one could. As far as I know, the main tenants were on a summer holiday at their bungalow by Lake Balaton, so the apartment was empty and you were seized by the excitement of what gave every promise of being an easy adventure. A light was on behind the garden gate at Logodi Street, so you couldn't evade the beady eye of the concierge, but then all your earlier expectations were dashed.

Yes.

The woman really did want a place to sleep. She had only

come out of inland security-service detainment a week before; others were living in her apartment. A woman friend had taken her in but had only been able to squeeze her into the kitchen, and the woman had felt that she couldn't spend another night jammed in "at the foot of the cooker," as I understand she said.

Yes.

Why should I be telling the story?

I couldn't tell any more myself.

True, it's a tale you've told many times now. It was on her that you based the waitress in Fiasco; she is also recognizable in The Union Jack; and you take final leave of her in some harrowing passages in Someone Else. How long was it that you lived together?

Forty-two years.

More than a generation... "She has gone, and she has taken with her the greater chunk of my life, the period in which creative work started and was completed, and also the period when, living in an unhappy marriage, we were so much in love with one another," as you write in Someone Else. A strange sentence...

Go on, carry on.

"Our love was like a deaf-mute child scampering with

*laughter on his face and arms outspread but whose mouth
slowly crumples into sobs because nobody understands him
and because he cannot ascertain the purpose of his scampering."[19] A truly sad metaphor, and even sadder is a short
passage that is to be found somewhat earlier in that volume:
"A mild late summer with A. [Albina]... to the Traunsee.
Balcony above the lake. However one looks at it (even out
of season), this is a first-class hotel, a loving gift to A. made
possible by the astounding twists my life has taken and the
opportunity they have created. She accepts it warily, with a
melancholy of something coming too late, an incorruptible
reserve demanded by fidelity to the bitterness of all the ir-
replaceable years; and I am seized over and over again with
terror because I have an almost palpable sense of something
irrevocable (perhaps what is commonly called destiny) and
for a person finally to yield to this recalcitrance of things is to
tempt a decline..." When was that remark recorded?*

The summer of 1994.

*In the following year, in 1995, she died... you yourself read
out an oration to those of your joint friends who were present at the funeral.*

Since a priest or rabbi was out of the question, whereas
a civilian official would only have parroted fatuous com-
monplaces...

*Let's turn back to Logodi Street to try to understand what
it was that brought the two of you together. After all, an
uncomfortable night does not obligate one in any way, and*

all that you write about her says more about the differences
between the two of you than the common ground: "I was
twenty-four, she was thirty-three," you write in Someone
Else. *"I had come back from the Nazi concentration camps,*
straight from the Endlösung, *and then the cheerless abyss*
of the harsh 'Fifties'—all of which, though there was not
yet the slightest sign of it at the time, was to have an in-
spirational rather than a deleterious effect on me. She too
had come from war, as a refugee, her family exterminated,
the family fortune—her inheritance—carried off. She had
made a new start; her husband had been locked up at the
outset of the show trials, her money and belongings con-
fiscated. She started over, then eventually she herself was
arrested and spent a year in captivity in prisons and intern-
ment camps. All that turned her against herself, broke her
confidence in the choices she made. Every choice she made—
including me, most especially me—was a self-punishment
for an arcane transgression she had never committed." An
interesting analysis, and if one bears in mind Jean Améry's
lost Weltvertrauen...

I don't believe it was that complicated. Both of us were
lonely and forlorn; we needed each other. Later on we
simply stayed together even when the absolute need may
have disappeared...

How did she end up in prison? What was the reason for
arresting her?

You have some very droll questions. We are talking about
1952, the baleful height of the Rákosi era. Why did they

arrest anyone during that period? Simply because the sphere of authority of those who made the arrests was unlimited and so they could arrest anyone at any time. A citizen living in a dictatorship who happens not to be in prison at that moment is merely a prisoner released on bail. In that context, the case itself, the "charge" on the pretext of which a person is arrested, is an anecdote of purely secondary importance.

And just as one fine day she was arrested, so on another fine day she was released.

In the wake of a speech made by Imre Nagy in July 1953, during his brief first period as premier, when the internment camps were opened up and deportees were released from the compulsory places of residence that were assigned to them.

Where did you yourselves live?

In rented accommodations, but it's not worth going into the story at this nadir. A rough and very boring period ensued that was preoccupied mainly by the foolish cares of sheer survival.

Until, one fine summer morning you "traversed half the city... with a four-wheeled tow cart," as one reads in The Union Jack.

It so happened that through some staggering bureaucratic marvel the authorities handed back to Albina the apartment that had been unlawfully sequestered from her. We piled the scanty appurtenances of our household onto a handcart and set off from the rented place on Lónyay Street in the Eighth District of Pest to take possession of the apartment on Török Street.[20]

The same as the one in which, roughly twenty-five years later, the "Old Boy" stood before the filing cabinet and thought.

Exactly. Of course, the filing cabinet was the product of an organic development over the ensuing decades.

A fairly intensive development if one considers merely the metamorphoses of the timbers, which had originally served as the linen drawer of a former divan-bed, then as a bookcase put together from that, as one can read in Fiasco. *But let's get back to the chronological order.*

That won't be easy.

Why?

Because it doesn't signify anything, The device of a sequence, of linearity, won't allow us to capture that darkest yet also most productive period of my life in the trap of narratability.

That is the period about which…

About which, as you yourself remarked not so long ago,

I am unable to give an account in the language of rationality.

*So, we are still stuck at the question of what happened to you
in the L-shaped corridor.*

No, we've already covered that. Like a sleepwalker I followed an inspiration that lured me further and further
from the everyday and about which I could have no idea
where it would lead ultimately. I stepped outside my history and was alarmed to notice that I was on my own. It
did not make things any easier that around this time we
were living off Albina's earnings alone.

*I can roughly understand your anxieties. "I always had a
secret life, and that was always the real one," you write in
Galley Boat-Log.[21] Much earlier you recorded more impas-
sively, even a little bit cynically: "The idea that anyone at
all might understand my secret occupation and the way of
life it entails is so alien to me that I am quite capable, even
unprompted, of joking about myself to anybody else without
feeling in the least ridiculous."[22]*

Yes, after a while one toughens up. On top of that, I had
to settle in for the long haul.

*It's interesting that right from the start you pictured yourself
as a sort of "outlaw writer." As someone living in a hostile
environment and engaged in a secret activity. What's the
explanation for that?*

Quite simply the fact that I *was* living in a hostile environment and engaged in a secret activity.

Don't you think that your general distrust may have been founded on a lack of self-confidence?

It's possible. Whatever it was founded on, I could not have imagined, and even today could not imagine, a "legal" art which was on harmonious terms with its social milieu.

Which makes it quite superfluous for me to pose the question: Did it never occur to you to get going on what is regarded as the "regular" route of publishing shorter-length stories to begin with in order to enter literary life, so-called, and generally just get your name more widely known?

That is, indeed, a prototypically superfluous question... I can't even say that I didn't wish to enter so-called literary life; the idea of entering it, that I could enter or might enter, simply didn't cross my mind... indeed, it didn't even cross my mind that what I was engaged on at home, between four walls, was what is called literature, and that literature had an organizational structure: the Writers' Association, the Ministerial Literary Department or Section, the Book Publishers' Administration, the Party artistic and literary... OK, I'll leave it at that. All I wanted to do was indicate that I was nevertheless well aware, incidentally, that we were living in a totalitarian state, and that had its own characteristics that it does no harm to think through if one is going to write a novel... indeed, that novel-writing will stall until one does think them through. All the more so, as it was precisely those characteristics that I wanted to write about, and right there one comes up against the first big question: Is that at all possible?

If I understand you right, it's a matter of one's world-view.

Precisely. And that is the way in which it presented itself to me: If power is totalitarian, and the accommodation to it is total, then *for whom* is one to portray man dominated by totalitarianism? And why should one portray him so dismissively, so negatively? For what kind of mysterious entity would the novel-writer work? Who would be left and be in a position to judge outside of the totality; indeed, this being a novel, who would derive amusement and learn from the work, and what is more, draw from it the conclusions about *works that were to come?* Who would be that personified or divinely abstract Archimedean centre of mass? The absurdity lies in the fact that since God died, there has been no objective gaze; we live in a state of *"panta rhei"*: everything is in flux, there is no foothold, and yet we still write as though there were, or rather as if, despite all appearances, there still existed a viewpoint *sub species aeternitas*, the divine standpoint, or the "eternal human" where the resolution of this paradox lies.

I begin to understand why you said that you needed time, more time, in fact a great deal more time.

Yes, it's not sufficient simply to pose these questions; you first have to get to them.

I note that the unfavourable reality did not seem to have any influence on your intellectual activities. From The Union Jack, *for instance, we learn that in the midst of living with the vexations of rented accommodation and all the other difficulties your life was turned upside-down most of all by a book that you found by complete chance among the bric-a-brac left behind in the Török Street apartment. Indeed, you go so far as to say that the book a person has need of almost unfailingly comes to hand, whether by design or fortuitously.*[23] *That was how you came across* The Blood of the Walsungs...

I thought at first I was holding the libretto for the *Ring*. As you know, I was a fanatical Wagner enthusiast at the time.

But when you opened it you found, instead of Wagner's text, the short story by Thomas Mann. Tell me, did the book really have such a decisive impact on your life?

It did, but now you have to imagine the intellectual wasteland of the Stalinist era. Radical literature was represented by *Volokolamsk Highway* and *Far from Moscow*...[24] I, on the other hand, needed to read the whole of world literature, as I soon realized. I hadn't the slightest idea how to set about it. Anyway, in a second-hand bookshop I bought a cheap paperback in the dog-eared pages of which modestly lurked Paul Valéry's hyperrefined essay on Leonardo da Vinci.[25] I couldn't understand a word, which impressed me hugely.

Paul Valéry—to my generation he is at best just a name.

Yet he's an important writer. The volume started right away with the letters he wrote about *The Crisis of the Mind*. In that Stalinist dictatorship, whoever would have thought there was a crisis of the mind? We had long passed that point without having given it a thought... or just listen to what he has to say about the poet's method: "The true condition of a genuine poet differs completely from the dreaming state... I presume to discern in it a purely conscious search, a polishing of thoughts, the clapping of the spirit into exquisite fetters, a constant triumph of the victim... Even he who wishes to record a dream has to do this when fully alert. If I wish to write down accurately the oddities, the self-contradictions, of the frail slumberer whom I was only just before, to follow this pensive plunge of the soul into my own depths, like the fallen leaf of a tree through the hazy infinitude of memory, it is not permissible to delude myself that I have managed to reach this without an intense straining of the consciousness, whose masterpiece will be that it also espies the thing which came into being only at its expense." Lines like that truly drove me wild. I soon made the acquaintance of two gentlemen who would regularly visit the same cafés that I called on: a Mr. Vermes, known from his diminutive mouse head and disproportionately large, translucent ear flaps as Bat-ears, and Mr. Weisz, who was known in Budapest's ever-inventive argot—after the title of Lajos Zilahy's early novel[26]—Something's-Adrift-in-the-Vise.

They were one-time booksellers who, after their businesses were taken into state ownership, used to lug what was left of their merchandise under their arms or in battered, old-fashioned briefcases. They managed to procure anything you ordered from them. By good fortune, I still had a few first editions of P. Howard's books that had remained, heaven knows how, from my childhood collection of books. That was a pseudonym that "cloaked," as was widely known, the popular Hungarian writer Jenő Rejtő, a writer blessed with a quirky sense of humour who in fact had been killed during the war while he was on forced labour service[27] on the Russian front. His books were officially prohibited, but at the time they were of considerable value, so that instead of paying ready money I used to barter with them. To cut a long story short, I was by then in some measure inwardly prepared for a literary encounter with a great author, and it was my luck that of all books it should have been precisely *The Blood of the Walsungs* that fate delivered into my hands. It was not just the boldness of its topic, incest, which fascinated me, but also the silky-smooth style, the irony, the melancholy, the *knowledge*… you can imagine how I was affected on reading lines like: "Creation! How did one create?… it came to him as in a yearning vision that creation was born of passion and was reshaped anew as passion. He saw the pale, spent woman hanging on the breast of the fugitive to whom she gave herself, he saw her love and her distress and he knew: so life must be to be creative"—who else was the text addressed to if not to me?

I totally understand.

Death in Venice came into my hands not much later, and I can say of that that it truly did change my life.

In what respect?

In the most extreme, I might say revolutionary sense, because in *Death in Venice* I was made to understand definitively that literature is a bottomless turmoil, a blow to the heart from which there is no recovery; an elemental courage and encouragement, and at the same time something like a fatal disease.

If I'm not mistaken, you have already mentioned that you were an incorrigible romantic whom the world of existing socialism all of a sudden clasped to its bosom. Did you have any other comparable literary epiphany?

Just one. During the 1957 Book Week in Budapest I was loafing fairly lost among the publisher's stands hunting for something new, and what's more something that I could afford. A yellow-backed little volume came to my hand: an unfamiliar book by a French author with a name that was unknown to me. While standing there I read a few sentences before looking at its jacket: it was priced at 12 forints.

Camus's novel, The Stranger, I believe?

Yes. And that was the second fatal blow for me. I didn't get over it for years.

What about Kafka?

I discovered his immeasurable greatness too late, at an age when one is less receptive to primary great experiences. I have the book-publishing policy of the Socialist era to thank for first attempting to hide Kafka from readers, then pooh-poohing him, and finally, when they got round to publishing him, stowing him away under the counter.

So, the bounds of your literary taste were determined by two such radically contrasting writers as Albert Camus and Thomas Mann. I would add Thomas Bernhard as well.

With every justification. It is possible to like Bernhard hugely for a while, but then you more readily put his books to one side. But aren't we being a bit too literary?

Probably, but then it is part of the subject.

True, true. What I was wondering was why I feel so uneasy about that expression you used: the bounds of your literary taste.

And have you puzzled it out?

There is something arbitrary about it that doesn't correspond to the facts. We seem to be leafing about in an enormously hefty book, entitled "Literature," and I stab a finger at two authors: they are my literary taste. In reality, however, it didn't happen like that. Both authors burst into my life like a catastrophe, and I'm using that word in the original sense of a disastrous overturning.

It's true that I picked the authors, but I couldn't help picking them.

Notwithstanding the fact that they fell into your hands by chance?

The word "chance" doesn't mean anything; it doesn't explain anything. I could replace it with the word "inevitable" and would be saying the same thing even though the two words bear apparently contrary meanings.

True. So we are still looking for an explanation as to what it was that held you prisoner among your papers.

Though sober common sense told me that I was pointlessly wasting my time and living a parasitic existence, and I took both those arguments deadly seriously... much later on, something Sartre says, most probably in *Words*, often went through my mind: "You talk in your own language but you write in a foreign one."[28] That sentence was not yet known to me, and I felt a little like someone who may well have left the tower of Babel but had not yet arrived anywhere.

Can you be more specific about what you mean by the "tower of Babel"?

A situation in which it's not just one another's languages that we don't understand but not even our own.

And that was precisely what you were looking for?

So I supposed, but in truth what I was looking for was that third language which is not mine, nor that of others, but the one in which I had to write, only I hadn't the slightest idea of that at the time, so that the more "immediately" I sought to write, the more false the resulting text.

Let's skip ahead. Do you make a habit of reading the reviews of your books?

Off and on, and only with due circumspection.

What do mean by "circumspection"?

You know, it takes a lot of confidence to have a book published. To "bring it out"—the expression itself indicates its gravity. You might also say that you hand it over.

Unless, that is, you wish to be a secret writer, you have no choice.

Precisely. On the one hand, you have to be aware that you are surrendering yourself completely, yet on the other that is exactly what you are aiming at. You therefore find yourself in an ironic situation. There is a need for circumspection because you will never be able to approach your own work through someone else's eyes— least of all a critic's eyes.

Yet you still sometimes read reviews. Why?

Human foible. But also because it can sometimes be instructive, especially in a society that has been riven so much by censorship, ideologies, and jockeying for position. Here in Hungary, literary criticism has become a genre in its own right, often having little or nothing to do with the work that happens to be under discussion—a lyrical genre, more poetic than poetry.

Is that your take on it? After decades of your name being barely known, suddenly in 2003 books, monographs, are being published about you in Hungary.

I wouldn't like to seem ungrateful, but in no case did I have the feeling that the books were really about me, still less about my works.[29]

Do you have the feeling that these people don't understand you?

I don't understand them. We speak different languages, hold different values. But for my own part I would rather end any discussion on the subject of literary criticism: it is unproductive and tedious.

Despite that, over time your existence as an author nevertheless loomed before you as a potentially soluble problem—or so at least the following cadence from Kaddish for an Unborn Child *would appear to suggest: "I am at most still a bit of a literary translator, if I am and have to be anything. As such, despite the threatening circumstances, in the end I*

radically removed from my path the ignominious existence
of a successful Hungarian author, even though, as my wife
(for a long time now someone else's wife) told me, I have
all the endowments it takes to be one (which slightly horri-
fied me at the time), not that she was saying, my wife said,
that I should jettison my artistic or any other principles, she
was merely saying, my wife said, that I should not be faint-
hearted, and the more that I was so, that is to say the less I
were to do that (jettison my artistic or any other principles),
the harder I would have to strive to realize those principles,
which is to say, when all is said and done, myself, and hence
to succeed, my wife said, since everyone strives for that, even
the world's greatest authors, 'Don't delude yourself,' my wife
said, 'if you don't want success, then why bother writing at
all?' she asked, and that is undoubtedly a thorny question,
but the time is not yet ripe for me to digress on that; and the
sad thing is that she probably saw straight into my heart,
she was probably absolutely right, I probably do (did) have
all the endowments it takes for the ignominious existence of
a successful Hungarian author... what is more, and even
more dangerous, I had within me in even greater measure
the flair needed for the equally ignominious existence of a
Hungarian author who is not successful, indeed unsuccessful—and here again I find myself clashing with my wife,
who again was the one who got it right, because once one
steps onto the path of success then one will be either successful or unsuccessful, there is no third way, though certainly
both are equally ignominious, albeit in different ways, which
is why, for a while, I escaped altogether, as a surrogate for al-
coholism, into the objective stupors of literary translation..."
I can see you are laughing...

Go on, admit it! I hit the nail on the head... But then, *Kaddish* in its entirety is fiction.

Still, a fiction that you wrote while living in a dictatorship, even if it was a late phase of that dictatorship. Give or take the odd irony, though, you did describe very accurately the dilemma faced by a writer, an intellectual of any sort, in a closed society.

One where at all events it is shameful to live. On account of my latest novel, *Liquidation*, I was leafing through *Kaddish* not long ago and I myself was taken aback by the frankness of the death wish which was the original stimulus, the guiding principle, for the novel.

In Galley Boat-Log *you are preoccupied quite a lot with the idea of suicide, as if you felt uneasy that survivors like Borowski, Améry, or Primo Levi eventually succumbed to this temptation...*

Do you think that "temptation" is really the right word here?

That's a question I'd rather put to you. The odd entry in that diary sounds almost like an apology, and I'm not thinking here of that oft-quoted self-reflection of yours in which you explain that what saved your life was the fact that you were pitched from a Nazi dictatorship straight into a Stalinist dictatorship, so that unlike others living in the free world you were never enticed by hope.[30] What struck me more were tucked-away remarks like: "In certain cases suicide cannot be condoned: it shows a lack of respect, as it were, to the wretched."[31]

Well yes, to survive Auschwitz—a trifle vulgar, perhaps. I might say it stands in need of an explanation.

Toward the end of an essay on Jean Améry you call him "the saint of the Holocaust."

A life that had been consummated and bore witness; moreover he knew exactly when it was time to cross into the apotheosis.

You can't mean you envy him?

Wonderment is always tinged with a tiny spot of envy. In any event, he gave a form to his life that I have not had the strength for.

Was Améry's example, or his figure, an inspiration for you in creating Bee, the antihero of your most recent novel, Liquidation?

I keep a photograph of him. He is sitting on a bench in a public space, his arms spread apart on the backrest. He is smiling. I have never seen such a smile anywhere else.

I know which photograph you mean; I have it too. Apart from the bitterness, there is indeed something otherworldly about it, if I may put it like that.

But to answer your question, while I was writing the novel I took the photo out many a time, sometimes studying it for as long as half an hour.

With the chilly inquiring look of a writer, or the unremitting pangs of guilt of the private individual?

I don't know how the person is separable from the writer, or the other way round. In any case I always strive to find the uniquely authentic interpretation.

The individual's interpretation as a writer?

That of the individual and of the situation.

Would you say "truth" instead of "interpretation"?

I don't know what the truth is. I don't know whether it is my job to know what the truth is, in any case. Truth-telling artists generally prove to be bad artists. Anyone who is right generally proves not to be right. We need to have respect for man's fallibility and ignorance; there is nothing sorrier than a person who is right...

I think I catch your drift. From the viewpoint of the end of the story, you have reached your goal and you were right.

Then there is no point in our continuing this discussion. That it is, so to say, over from a dramaturgical point of view; now let's see what story comes of it.

Well... the story of a hard yet successful literary career.

Right then, let's now look at how the success story and the life that I undertook to interpret relate to each other.

Obviously, the result of a first, superficial look will be absurd.

What do you understand by that notion, by "absurd"?

That what's on the outside has little to do with what's on the inside.

Or, in other words, the story to real life.

Nevertheless, there is something in common to the extent that your novels stem from your existence, and the result stems from your novels...

With the rider that those novels became detached from me earlier on, so they're no longer the novels they were at the time of writing: hazardous, seemingly unrealizable enterprises.

Fine, but the jackpot still depends on the spin of the wheel at the roulette table, not on any decisions, struggles, or conflicts that the player may have undergone beforehand.

That's not a bad simile. I would only draw your attention to the difficulties of narratability; it may be no chance that Homer was supposed to be a blind man. If we do not know what we are narrating, then we soon get to the incommensurable relation of existence and the seemingly achieved goals, where we have to abandon everything. Furthermore, this logical dead-end has been reached in the name of logic.

And if logic were to be suspended?

That still seems to be the most useful method. Then I can see my life as a series of now rational, now absurd struggles—stations that I am not permitted to thread onto the string of expediency because then I shall obtain a false result.

Despite that, you were led by goals; you must surely have set yourself a goal of some kind while you stepped from one station to the next.

Very likely, but then that's a rule of life: a man lives with his face turned to the future, but that does not mean to say that he moves forward. I accept that we may be guided by notions of goals, but that is just an illusion: what we imagine to be the future is not as yet reality itself. It is not the future that lies in wait for us but the next moment, and anyone who thinks he is seeing beyond that moment is deceiving himself.

All of us live in this productive state of self-deception most of the time.

No doubt. And in the meantime lose sight of the ultimate goal.

I see too much Schopenhauer on your bookshelves.

Every great philosophy is a philosophy that serves to conquer the fear of death, but the truly great philosophies conquer the fear of death by accepting death.

Does the thought of suicide still occupy you?

It does, but in a different way than before, during the dictatorship, when it seemed to be the only alternative...

Would you care to finish the sentence?

Certainly: in face of the shame of continued survival.

Would it be right to say, then, that the comforting thought of suicide helped keep you alive?

A marvellous paradox! I never put it to myself in quite those terms.

Yet I was just going to ask you to what degree this incessant toying with the idea of suicide is serious, and if it is, then to what extent has it altered the prospect for you.

Are you asking about the sorts of techniques I have employed to play for time; what, in the final analysis, was my method for surviving; or to put it another way, what did I use, and how, to deceive myself? If I were to say that I always wanted to die, and instead of that I always wrote a book—that would be an elegant cop-out, wouldn't it?

I would make do with it if I were to read it in a book by an aphorist like Cioran, but with you I'm expecting a genuine response.

I'm not sure that if some less brutal means had been lying to hand, morphine, let's say, or some other reliable poison... well, I'm not sure whether, on one or two occasions, my life might have been in serious jeopardy. In a western democracy I would not have come to know those moods of despair on which my heuristics fed. On the other hand, the other day, while organizing the notes that I made for *Liquidation*, I came across a slip of paper... hang on a second, I'll find it in a moment... here it is. "Those years once more, the depressing dictatorship mood, happy deliberations of suicide, the whole death-game of the Seventies and Eighties..."

I see what you mean: a bit morbid, but fathomable. The discreet charms of the dictatorship... Did you ever talk about such things with Albina?

No, no way! We had other things to do: one had to live.

Could she not have found a better, easier occupation for herself than working as a waitress?

No. I mentioned, didn't I, that her first husband had been put to use in one of the show trials, and the sentence he received included confiscation of all his property? Albina was obliged to leave their big middle-class home straight away and urgently sort out a means of livelihood. She had acquired no profession, but she did have a driving licence, which meant that she managed to obtain a job as a truck driver with TEFU, the state haulage company. She worked alongside other, likewise "*déclassé* elements" as well as a few genuine professional truck drivers in handling what counted as the almost punitive business of making the dawn deliveries of vegetables and milk, which amounted to stopping each and every time for the produce to be unloaded in front of the shops. She made a fairly conspicuous figure with her long, lacquered fingernails from her previous mode of life, not to say the Alsatian dog that she took along with her on the trips because there was nobody with whom the animal could be left. The dog would obligingly leap up onto the back of the truck, but once it was up there it would also "guard" the truck, so the loading workers wouldn't dare go near it.

I can just picture the bizarre scene.

Not long after we had got together she found herself a job with what was called the Restaurant and Buffet Company. In those days that was a major privilege; the firm was managed by a former footballer called Lajos Ónodi, who collected a whole flock of *déclassé* persons who had been dislodged from their old ways of life. There was a dishwasher who had been a countess and a baroness who had been promoted to cocktail waitress, a football player's wife whose husband had left her—take your pick. Albina was given a job as a waitress in the

Abbázia [Opatija] Restaurant which used to be by the Oktogon.

While in the meantime you sat at home reading Schopen-hauer.

One could put it like that.

Did you, in all honesty, read right through all four of the hefty volumes of the Hungarian edition?

Of *Parerga and Paralipomena*, you mean? I certainly did; indeed, for a time it was a constant reading-matter, and that had the abiding merit that it led me on to Kant.

Another of the books that you had need of and that sure enough, found their way into your hands?

Exactly. To the best of my recollection, a new Hungarian translation of the *Critique of Pure Reason* was published in the Sixties. I bought it, but it lay around unread for who knows how long. It was just as much a mystery why I packed it in the suitcase when Albina and I went down to Balatonalmádi one summer. Brilliant July sunshine gave way to days of rain. One could step out of the room that we had rented onto a covered wooden balcony. I dipped into the book and then couldn't put it down. I read it the same way that I had read Agatha Christie's detective stories when I was young. It was further reinforced by the fact, which I had long suspected anyway, that the world is not "an objective reality independent of us," as the Marxists would harp on, but quite the opposite: it exists only as long as I exist, and it only exists in the manner in which I can imagine it: in the midst of the conditions of space and time and causal relations that are given to me.

A lot of that has since been refuted, if I'm not mistaken.

That's of no concern to me; for that great text corroborated and rescued me completely. Why would I be interested in facts? Kant cannot be refuted any more than an oak tree can be refuted. It grew and spread and it stands there, but there are times when we need it in order to stay in its shade and marvel at it, like at a great encouraging example.

That sounds rather like a credo, which is quite unusual coming from you. So, as you have already mentioned, in 1960 you start writing Fatelessness. *You were thirty years old at the time and, on the evidence of the photographs, a determined young man in good shape, who, according to what is in effect the final chapter of* Fiasco, *does not wish to take the chance to escape "from this city which denied all hope, this life that belied all hope: 'Where to?' asked Köves, at a loss to understand,... 'Does it matter?' Sziklai fumed. 'Anywhere!' ... He set off again. 'Abroad,' he added, and in Köves's ears the word, at that instant, sounded like a festive peal of bells. He walked on for a while without a word, his head hung in thought, by Sziklai's side. 'Sorry, but I can't go,' he said eventually. 'Why not?' Sziklai again came to a*

*stop, astonishment written all over his face. 'Don't you want
to be free?' he asked. 'Of course I do,' said Köves. 'The only
trouble is,' he broke into a smile, as if by way of an apology,
'I have to write a novel.' 'A novel?!' Sziklai was dumbstruck.
'Now of all times?. . . You can write it later, somewhere else,'
he went on. Köves continued smiling awkwardly: 'Yes, but
this is the only language I know,' he worried. 'You'll learn
another one,' Sziklai said, waving that aside. . . 'By the time
I learn one I'll have forgotten my novel.' 'Then you'll write
another one,' Sziklai's voice by now sounded almost irritated, and it was more for the record than in hope of being
understood that Köves pointed out: 'I can only write the one
novel that it is given me to write'. . . They stood wordlessly,
facing each other in the street, a storm of shouts of 'We want
to live!' around them, . . . then they swiftly embraced. Sziklai
was then swallowed up in the crowd, whereas Köves turned
on his heels and set off back at a shambling pace, like someone who is in no hurry as he already suspects in advance all
the pain and shame his future holds for him." I have deliber-
ately quoted from this scene because, for all its grotesqueness,
I nevertheless feel it is very true to life.*

Rightly so. I think all big decisions are, in truth, as gro-
tesque as that.

I wonder why.

Because they are inexplicable. You have to choose between bombast and silence.

I have the feeling that in light of The Union Jack *there is no need for us to say anything more about 1956. The late Sixties were characterized by a national collective amnesia, the emergence of a Hungarian society which was derided as "goulash communism" that you yourself have referred to, here and there, as "the intellectual swamp of the Brezhnev era" or "the West's favourite brand of Communism."*

Yes, that was when I noticed the emergence of a collective morality (or rather immorality) of the functional man, and of fatelessness.

In Galley Boat-Log one can read lengthy analyses[32] about this discovery, about functional man being "an insubstantial being at the mercy of totalitarianism." Then in Liquidation one of the characters speaks about a separate "species" of survivors: "...we are all survivors; that is what determines our perverse and degenerate mental world. Auschwitz. Then the forty years that we have put behind us since." What I am particularly interested in, right now, is what you mean by a "collective morality."

That peculiarly Hungarian consensus that blossomed in the name of survival and, in essence, was founded on an "acceptance of realities," so-called.

Realities that included the Kádár regime, installed after the crushing of the 1956 revolution...

Yes, that cheap conformity that undermined every moral and intellectual stand, that petit-bourgeois police state that called itself socialist but which regarded that docile and corrupt, simpering and authoritarian, mind-numbing, semifeudal, semi-Asiatic, militaristic Horthyite society, governed from the handsomely built dictator's waistcoat pocket, as its true model.

According to the witticism of the day, Hungary still counted as "the happiest barrack in the socialist camp."

If I were really looking to be ironic, I would call it the country that, in the course of its historical evolution, lived through enlightened absolutism in the late eighteenth century and has now got as far as liberal totalitarianism.

"World time," you write in Galley Boat-Log, *"that blindly ticking machine, which has been dropped in the quagmire hereabouts and is now overrun by masses of sprightly Lilliputians, who are busy trying to dismantle the appliance, or at least silence it."*[33]

And in so doing provincial stillness set in; the stillness of the Kádár regime.

Still, perhaps even that had its good side, didn't it? You need stillness to write a novel, don't you?

That's one way of looking at it: one could pull oneself back as far as was possible. That was one of the reasons I stayed in Hungary at the end of 1956: the low cost of living and a safe hiding place. Albina pleaded that we should go...

May one ask if you ever regretted not listening to her?

You may ask, but there is no answer.

You have said that it was the language, first and foremost, that bound you to Hungary; but then, on the other hand, what has become clear so far is that you gained your most stunning literary experiences, virtually without exception, from foreign writers, whether in good or bad translation. Did no Hungarian traditions have an impact on you?

It seems not. Only later did I become acquainted with Gyula Krúdy and Dezső Szomory, whose prose I greatly love and admire; Géza Ottlik or Iván Mándy, or indeed even Sándor Márai, whose books were available only as contraband items, were still unknown to me.

Does that go any way to explaining the foreignness of the language of Fatelessness?

No, the foreignness of the language of *Fatelessness* is explained solely by the foreignness of the subject and the narrator.

What I seeking for an answer to is how you "managed" so totally to marginalize yourself in the intellectual life of Hungary that you could hardly be said to have been present at "the sidelines," to use one of Iván Mándy's categories.

During the Kádár era that was more or less the limit of my ambition.

If one pays close attention, certain pages of Galley Boat-Log *attest to the fact that your unnatural situation took a greater toll on you than you may have been prepared to admit even to yourself.*

You know, there's a kind of syndrome to which I have given the name "dictatorship schizophrenia." Every artist longs for recognition, though he is well aware that it is precisely what he doesn't want. He finds it hard, however, to resign himself to the fact that he has created a work of art that nobody takes any notice of. One incident that happened to me was that an unknown colleague addressed me in the corridor of the writer's retreat at Szigliget. He must have arrived not long before, because I hadn't seen him around. "Are you Imre Kertész?" "Yes, I am." "You wrote *Fatelessness?*" "I did." Whereat, he embraced me and rained kisses on my cheeks—he was a tall and beefy man, so I had a job pulling myself away from him. He lauded the book at length, and in a far from unintelligent way. It was only then that I discovered who his nibs was: one of the Party's chief ideologists, a chief censor, what was then called a super-Reader, the highest court of appeal in matters of suspect manuscripts. He was editor-in-chief of some critical journal in which, following his abounding enthusiasm, he got an anonymous author to write a noncommittal review that was printed in a well-hidden corner of the journal devoted to brief notifications of insignificant books.

Nice! But what can one learn from the story that one didn't know already?

As best I recall, you asked me how I had managed to "marginalize" myself in the intellectual life of Hungary. As you can see, I didn't have to try too hard. The Kádár regime's scale of values functioned like a well-oiled machine, more or less automatically, quite independent even of the people who operated it. Orwellian double-think was so self-evident a feature of life in Hungary that it could not be shaken by any private convictions or opinions.

So how could personal convictions or opinions exist, or indeed be articulated?

By totally separating them from the "must-know" region of the brain, the sphere of practical action. The blame for any consequences of that could be shifted onto the existing world order, the dictatorship, so nobody personally felt themselves as being dishonest.

Or crazy.

Quite the reverse, since they had pragmatic sense on their side; in Hungary, only life's cavillers and dissidents could be crazy.

I found an intriguing entry in Galley Boat-Log *in which, back in 1964, you wrote down a quotation both in the original English and in Hungarian translation: "He was a lonely ghost uttering a truth that nobody would ever hear. But so long as he uttered it, in some obscure way the continuity was not broken. It was not by making himself heard but by*

staying sane that you carried on the human heritage." And
you end by attributing it to Shakespeare.

It's actually Orwell.[34]

But you wrote Shakespeare, presumably out of caution.

"Dictatorship schizophrenia," as I said. In case my note-
books were gone through.

Those written traces of the struggle you were waging for
your intellectual self-preservation.

Those notes were enormously important for me at the
time.

And also to preserve your sanity. As I see it, that was ul-
timately the most difficult thing of all for you in the Kádár
world: to keep a level head. If there is any poetry in Galley
Boat-Log *then it springs from the struggle you were waging*
to keep a sane mind... But let's now switch to light enter-
tainment. Would you care to say how you became the au-
thor of the book for a number of much-performed musicals,
popular light comedies?

It's been done to death. I've already covered that a hundred times.

I came across the following lines in the frame novel of
Fiasco: *"I wrote a novel, in the meantime producing dia-*
logues for musical comedies, each more inane than the last,

in order to make a livelihood (hoodwinking my wife who, in the semi-gloom of the theatre auditorium at "my premieres," would wait for me, wearing the mid-grey suit that had been specially tailored for me for such occasions, to take my place before the curtains in a storm of applause, and she would imagine that our beached life would finally work free itself from the shoals after all); but I, after assiduously putting in appearances at the pertinent branch of the National Savings Bank to pick up the not inconsiderable royalties due for this claptrap, would immediately sneak home with the guilty conscience of a thief to write a novel anew..." That makes it sound rather as though writing farces became your real job and you considered novel-writing a form of truancy, of bunking-off from school.

As indeed it was. In practice, I wouldn't have been able to give an excuse for it that was any better than I could have given for stamp-collecting or breeding exotic birds.

Was that because you were lacking in self-confidence, or more because you suspected that you would be unable to convince those around you?

Incontrovertibly, I lack a prophet's powers of persuasion. But then what could I have said? Just wait and you'll find out just who I am? Meanwhile just be so kind as to carry on fending for me.

But she was your wife, and she loved you?

When it comes down to it, in the end we are on our

own, and there can be no kidding oneself in that respect. "A painter paints a picture with the same feeling as that with which a criminal commits a crime," Degas said.[35] Once I start to work the world becomes my enemy...

That certainly sounds rather hard-nosed. Incidentally, I heard that not so long ago one of the Budapest theatres offered to stage one of your old pieces.

I had a hard job talking them out of it.

Why wouldn't you agree to the staging?

Look, at the time they were written those pieces had a single practical purpose: making a livelihood. As far as their intellectual content is concerned, if I may put it this way, not a molecule comes from me.

Where on earth did you get the idea of earning money from light comedy pieces, anyway?

I've already mentioned that I was one of a small circle of ambitious young people who, at the height of the Stalinist era, used to analyze the plays of Ferenc Molnár.

Sziklai, the comedy writer protagonist of Fiasco, *went abroad...*

My friend, Kállai, on the other hand, one of life's flesh-and-blood heroes, stayed in Budapest. And he realized

his dream by becoming a well-known playwright, one
of whose plays had an uninterrupted run of four hundred performances in one of the city theatres. To keep
the story short, he turned up at our Török Street flat
one freezing afternoon in the winter of 1957–58, pushed
aside the papers, sharpened pencils, and erasers that
were spread out on my wonky table, and reminded me
that a few years before I had told him about a four-hand
comedy set in a single scene. Had I written it down? The
hell I had written it down! Then I should do so, and be
quick about it. I haven't got the time; I'm writing a novel.
The two are not mutually exclusive. What was the matter: Did I want to die of starvation? That's a powerful
reason, but I don't know how to write a play. We'll write
it together. But what if I simply can't get my head round
doing it: for instance, just can't hit upon a plot? We'll just
have to hit upon one together!

And did you?

We did. After that I was able to write the dialogues off
my own bat.

But why was the piece so urgent?

A fair few actors were banned from making regular
stage appearances after the 1956 Uprising. Some of them
looked around for other occupations, whereas others
banded together into casual "companies" and diligently
went round the country, hiring local halls and performing

some harmless play. A four-hander comedy that played in a single scene would fit into even a small café.

I see. And the cultural authorities didn't raise any objections?

Quite the reverse. The by then gradually stabilizing Kádár regime had need of laughter, of light, apolitical entertainment, a Kakanian peacetime mood. Revolting, isn't it?

That it is. So your pieces, with their "happy endings," contributed to upholding the conformity that you radically disavowed via your literary works and your entire lifestyle.

That's a well-organized dictatorship for you! The need to make a livelihood turned me into a collaborator.

"Life is either a demonstration or a collaboration," you write in Liquidation.

That's what I mean. One day I would demonstrate by writing my novel, the next day collaborate by writing bilge. That just underlines one thing I said earlier: the scale of values of the Kádár world spread to everyone and everything, just like an epidemic. No one was exempt or immune.

But seriously, did writing these skits cause you real soul-searching?

Not at all! I looked on it as a sort of prank by which I made a living.

So, you would turn up at the first nights then with all the scruples of a thief...

Exactly so.

How many of these plays did you write with your friend Kállai?

Four or five, I don't rightly recall.

After which you switched to translating.

But that was only possible after *Fatelessness* had been published.

So there was something for which you had Fatelessness *to thank... Did its rejection by the first publisher you approached surprise you?*

In point of fact, yes, but then again, not. It was somehow all of a piece with the things that usually happened to me.

Did it never occur to you that the assessment of those "experts," let's call them that, might have been right in some measure?

Nothing of the sort entered my head for a moment. It

was quite obvious that the letter from the publisher was baloney and the entire drift of the invective was to serve up a pretext for rejection of the manuscript.

So what did you do with the returned manuscript?

"For the time being" I put it in the filing cabinet.

You resigned yourself to the fact that the book was not going to be published?

I don't remember it coming to that.

All the same, what did you think or feel?

Boundless disgust and self-reproach at having deserved the fate.

I read somewhere that James Joyce was able to boast of having received more than a hundred letters of rejection. For his Swann's Way, *the first volume of* In Search of Lost Time, *Proust was rejected by an editor by the name of André Gide at Gallimard...*

Those are not truly comparable instances. Joyce and Proust had to deal with the incomprehension and intellectual slothfulness that are customary with publishers. Those sorts of barriers one can understand and overcome. I, on the other hand, was rejected by the competent police body of a totalitarian regime, a censorship office disguised as a publisher that was run by an ex-officer of the military secret police. In my case it had long ceased being a matter of my book as such; it was a matter of a direct challenge to the Authority, of which cognizance is cursorily taken, while the perpetrator is simply swept aside as a roadblock with a devastating flip of the odious authority's hand.

This is not just the way you were made to see it by the "dictatorship schizophrenia" to which you have already referred?

I don't think so.

Nevertheless, in the end another publishing house did take you on and publish the book.

Not just *another* but the *only* other publishing house. There were no others at that time, and anyway, that second publishing house could just as easily have rejected it as the first.

True.

There would have been no further options.

That's also true. Let's cast anchor in this extraordinary situation: one of the publishing houses has rejected your book but the other does not respond. What would have happened if the response from them were likewise negative? Would you have abandoned writing novels?

I don't think the question would ever have arisen in that form. At worst, I wouldn't have bothered searching any more for a publisher for my manuscript.

Let me go back to a remark you made just before about the possibility of your book being seen as a direct challenge to the Authority. Do you mean in regard to its "subject" as such, the Holocaust, or the way in which you handle it in Fatelessness?

The sheer impudence that the book denoted through its mere existence, its style, its independence; a sarcasm inherent in its language that strains permitted bounds and dismisses the craven submissiveness that all dictatorships ordain for recognition and art.

Going through that early "intermission" period in Galley Boat-Log, *I come across an outline of another important recognition you reached: "I am bringing up 'this subject,' so I am told, too late, it is no longer of topical interest. 'This sub-ject' should have been dealt with much earlier, at least ten years ago, etc. Yet these days I have again had to realize that the Auschwitz myth is the only thing which truly interests me... Whatever I think about, I am always thinking about Auschwitz. Even if I may seem to be talking about some-thing quite different, I am still talking about Auschwitz. I am a medium for the spirit of Auschwitz, Auschwitz speaks through me. Everything else strikes me as inane by compari-son... Auschwitz and everything bound up with it (but then what does not have something to do with it?) is the greatest*

trauma for the people of Europe since the Crucifixion..."[36]
*Do you still see it the same way now, several decades later
and after the change of regime in Hungary?*

With appropriate changes, yes.

What's changed?

Everything—the world, politics, you, me...

*Let's just see how much. Would you still mention Auschwitz
and the Crucifixion in the same sentence today?*

More than ever, because it is precisely in that context
that Auschwitz's baleful significance is revealed for those
who have grown up in Europe's ethical culture. One of
the laws enshrined in the Ten Commandments of that
culture is "Thou shall not kill." So in other words if mass
murder can become common practice, a day-to-day rou-
tine so to say, then one needs to decide the validity of
the culture for which an illusory value system has taught
every single one of us in Europe, from primary school
onward, to be murderers and victims alike.

*That's a dreadful vision: million of schoolchildren, satch-
els on their backs, trudging to school only to be reunited
again as perpetrators and victims in the anterooms of the
crematoria and by the ditches dug as mass graves... Is that
what we have come to? Is that what this conversation is
about?*

It looks as though if we start to talk about culture and the European scale of values, we soon get round to the question of murder.

In one of your earlier essays you come to this conclusion: "The Holocaust, in essence, is not a historical event any more than, let's say, the idea that the Lord handed over to Moses on Mount Sinai a tablet of stone carved full of letters is a historical event."

Maybe I ought to have phrased it rather as "the Holocaust is not a *purely* historical event." The very fact that it is a historical event carries its own extraordinary importance, of course, just as the fact that it cannot be degraded to a purely historical event.

"The question," you write, "should run 'Can the Holocaust create any value?'" And before going on to sketch out a clear outline of the question, you make it understood well in advance: "If we examine whether the Holocaust is one of the vital issues of European civilization, of European consciousness, we shall find that indeed it is, because that same civilization must reflect on its being the one within whose framework that was carried out, otherwise it will itself become a casualty civilization, a crippled primitive being that is carried helplessly toward extinction." That was the essay about Jean Améry that you wrote in 1992 under the title "The Holocaust as Culture."[37]

I would write exactly the same today.

Do you mean to say that the question has still not been settled?

No, not at all—quite the contrary. It would be political blindness if one were to fail to notice at every hand the positive signs of this determination that has been reached in the consensus between the states of Europe.

I still get the feeling that you are holding back on something.

Look, one might add the remark that although an Auschwitz was indeed possible, the only response to that unique crime, a catharsis, has not been possible. That has been made impossible by reality, our mundane reality, the way in which we live our lives—or in other words, which made Auschwitz possible in the first place.

A pretty stringent comment, I would say... what, in your view, needs to happen in order that...

I don't know. I don't think it's me you should be asking.

In 2005, a Holocaust museum opened in Hungary, while in Berlin a controversial memorial to the Holocaust was unveiled. The sixtieth anniversary of the liberation of Auschwitz was marked around the world... it goes without saying that you too were invited to these ceremonies.

Certainly, many of the memorial sites honoured me with invitations, but I had to turn them all down.

May I ask why?

Because I didn't feel strong enough to go, and then I had a job holding back my aversion.

I would ask you to be a bit more precise in stating the reason, however harsh that may be.

I don't know if I am capable of that. The only people who were not besmirched by the shame of the Holocaust were the dead. It is painful to carry the brand of surviving for some unaccountable reason. You remained here so you could spread the Auschwitz myth; you remained here as a sort of freak. You are invited to attend anniversaries; your irresolute face is video-recorded, your faltering voice, you hardly notice that you've become a kitsch supporting character in a fraudulent narrative, and you sell for peanuts your own story, which bit by bit you yourself understand least of all. But instead of mourning your lost story, you complain about your daily food ration. You rake in the breast-beating remorse of the jubilee speeches because you believe the mass is being said for you, and you are late in noticing that you have already played your part and there is no longer any need for you here.

All the same, a few years ago you did visit Auschwitz.

Yes, in 2000 the German Academy chose to hold its regular annual meeting in Cracow, and I couldn't resist the occasion.

You wrote a memo there that you showed me when we started preparing for this conversation. Would you consider it an impertinence if I were to ask you to make that sheet public, as it contains nothing that it would be improper for others also to hear?

I've no objection.

It starts with the dateline: April 3rd, 2000. "With the German Academy to Cracow. Why did I travel on from there to Auschwitz-Birkenau? What was the dare to which I capitulated? What fed the vain sense of satisfaction that haunted me there? I went up into the control tower. The— how should I put this?—the style of the place both enthralled and appalled me. The desolate terrain, that mercilessly expedient landscape, said everything. I walked along the ramp, Magdi beside me. She was silent for the most part, both of us were, but still I was unable to shake off the feeling that I am walking along the ramp, M. beside me. It was a triumphal march, however I look at it. I had gravely offended the spirits of the dead. Was I sensible of this? Among the ruins of the crematorium an academic colleague, a somewhat conspicuously well-dressed German of around fifty, threw himself tearfully into my arms, and I held him as if I were able to bestow absolution on him. It was now that I truly recognized the grotesqueness of the place. I hastily got out, away, away, back to my home, into irredeemable survival from which I have no passage through to a past that is separated from me by barbed wire. Was I aware of this? Or had I simply forgotten? In any event the shame of this excursion will long haunt me..." By then Magdi had been your wife for four years, if I am not mistaken.

You are not mistaken. The wedding was in April 1996.

It roused a fair degree of interest in Budapest at the time. By then you were no longer an unknown author, while Magdi was heading an office for an American venture.

She represented the state of Illinois, setting up commercial and cultural links between Chicago and Budapest. She had returned "home" when Hungary was moving to a democratic system at the beginning of the Nineties, full of enthusiasm after having lived in Chicago for thirty-four years.

I recall a wonderful garden somewhere at the top of Rose Hill in Budapest.

That's right. M. was renting an apartment there at the time.

There were loads of guests. I arrived just when the ceremony was about to start: a Unitarian priestess was putting on her black cassock. That incidentally was something many people wondered about: Why Unitarian?

Possibly not everyone was aware of the significance of the ceremony. Consummation still invariably evokes for us God's name. Magdi had to move a long way from the country, and she returned from a long way away so that the two of us might meet, and she was not able to ascribe that to pure chance… as for me, one doesn't have to be a believer to be receptive to the wonders of life…

But why did you choose a Unitarian ceremony specifically?

May I remind you of what that priest once said to me: "God has no religion." And the Unitarians—in the person of the minister, Ilona Szentiványi—accepted the two of us: one a Roman Catholic, the other a Jew. We set off for Germany the next day: two weeks together in a hired car—that was the honeymoon. That was when the German translation of *Fatelessness* appeared.

Were you pleased about the… the…

Yes, it was hard for me, too, to hit upon my verbal relation to that undoubtedly absurd yet nonetheless amazing whatever…

Given that it's literature we're talking about in the final analysis, let us dare call it success.

OK, let's do that.

In 2003, the historian Jan Philipp Reemtsma, head of the Institute for Social Research in Hamburg, asked you to give the opening speech for the reopening of an exhibition under the title of "The Crimes of the Wehrmacht." In that lecture you spoke directly about the reluctant memory of the survivor. Let me quote you: "I have to admit that I too lived through some difficult days as I leafed through the exhibition catalogue. Had I forgotten, by any chance, that I myself was a participant in and survivor of these horrors? Had I forgotten the scent of dew-drenched daybreaks when the volleys of gunfire would crack? Sunday evenings in the camp barrack block, when the presumptive crematorium fodder were still able to dream about festive cakes? If I had not exactly forgotten, once I had transmuted it into words it had all burned out and somehow come to rest within me. Only grudgingly do I surrender that peace of mind." But then you have to surrender it after all when you come to the exhibition's pictures: "Ecce homo—behold a man. Is that him? One day he is called away from beside his wife, his children, his elderly parents, and the very next day he is shooting women, children, the elderly into a ditch, and with evident relish at that. How is that possible? Obviously with the aid of hatred, the hatred which, along with falsehood, has become an indispensable necessity, I might go so far as to say the most important psychological nutriment for mankind in our time..." "I sense hatred as an energy," you go on to say, "The energy is blind, but its source is exactly the same vitality from which creative forces take nourishment. Hatred, if it is well organized, creates a reality in the same way as even love might create a reality."

That is a utopia, of course, but there are times when I almost take it seriously.

You said about Liquidation, your most recent novel, that you were casting a final glance at Auschwitz as the lengthening of time is gradually closing down the horizon for you. It's true that never before have you painted quite such a godforsaken universe; equally, your world has not pulsed as much with a freedom that you can scent from almost each and every line like a light spring breeze.

The two may be closely interlinked.

In what way?

We have already spoken about the paradox that God may be found readily in a dictatorship, whereas in a democracy there is no longer any metaphysical excuse: the individual in his own right struggles with his freedom.

You are not suggesting that man is transcendent, his non-worldly life is a mere political issue, are you?

The issue is not political, but you pose it in two different ways in the two political systems—in the one as the sole option, in the other as one of the options.

You have used the word "myth" twice in connection with Auschwitz, and in a different sense on both occasions...

Spuriously so the second time; I noticed that myself.

By "myth" one usually denotes some fraudulent ideology, doesn't one?

I use the word in its original signification, in the sense of a total loss of values, in the way in which the mariners of ancient Greece on an island heard a harrowing cry of "Great Pan is dead!"

You clearly heard Nietzsche's call of "God is dead!"

It's true, we have to start all over again, from the beginning.

Is that really what Liquidation *is about?*

That is what all my works are about, isn't it?

And now that the trilogy of novels has expanded into a tetralogy, do you feel that your work is complete?

Trilogy, tetralogy—those terms say nothing to me. I just wrote the novel that had to be written, which always seemed to me just as fragile as my own stamina, even my own continuance. To employ an Adornoesque paraphrase: "To write a novel cycle after Auschwitz is barbaric."

So how did the term "trilogy"—designating by that the novels Fatelessness, Fiasco, *and* Kaddish for an Unborn Child—*become quite so commonly employed?*

I have no objection to it, whether it's a trilogy or tetralogy—that doesn't change anything. The truth is that with my work everything is connected with everything else, but those connections arise by an organic process without my having made them fit some premeditated literary box of tricks. They come out so unintentionally that I often surprise myself. Those are the rare lucid moments when one suddenly becomes aware that every line, every sentence one writes is operating in the force field of some sort of coherence from which we are able to surmise the presence of a more solid reality, of our genuine existence, lurking at the very bottom of our existence. That's sufficient for me to turn my back on the trilogy with a shrug of the shoulders.

Liquidation is anyway the first of your novels to be written in its entirety after the change in regime, indeed to use that as its subject.

It chose freedom as its subject.

Yes, but its world is still very much a typical late-Kádár-era world, I'd be interested to know where you drew your material from, given that you were then living very much in seclusion, not known in intellectual circles and, to my knowledge, you played no active role in the "democratic opposition," not putting a signature to any of the protest letters of the period...

They didn't get to me: it wasn't just them who didn't know me, but I didn't know them either.

So you would have signed them?

Most likely.

Out of sympathy?

Out of cowardice; so they would not consider me a coward.

That's a good one! Would you not have agreed with them?

Well, as far as their pragmatism was concerned—not at all. I was no fan of the reform Communists because I never thought that Brezhnev could be reformed, whereas there was no way I could imagine "socialism with a human face" when there were still "Soviet units temporarily stationed in our country." Whether it has a human face or not, socialism is malformed and repulsive. And then on top of that—and this is where it gets pickier—there was an overripe... an overripe playfulness, what I might call a latent cynicism, about the whole thing, as if people on both sides were respecting, as it were, well-known "rules of the game." The regime, the "establishment," displayed its amenability—the fact that it was at least respecting a liberal minimum—to advantage. Equally, though, the totalitarian power could have switched to "harsh methods" at any time. The chance that a person may be demeaned and become a scummy tool of the authority during the tortures, however, is for me a disproportionately high price for nothing.

And if I were to probe you on what your political convictions are, or do you in fact hold any such views...

Certainly I do. The trouble is just that its reality has passed, like that of, say, the Jasperian species of democracy or the liberal conservatism of an István Széchenyi.

Is it possible you are really sympathetic to conservative ideals?

Why not? If God existed, I would be pious. What is more, if there were a genuine conservative party in Hungary—which would probably constitute an even greater miracle than if God were to exist—I would be a sincere supporter.

Are you sure about that?

No, but I am sure that the prerequisites for a completely normal political life in Hungary are still only at an early stage.

What do you mean?

That the country needs, at long last, to get over the trauma caused by the change in regime: it needs to accept freedom—or more than that, rejoice in it.

Perhaps it's not as easy as that. After all, the new citizen in you crumbled the instant you caught sight of a customs officer's cap...

You're referring to my short story "Sworn Statement."

Yes, and that reminds me of several non-literary questions that I am unable to keep to myself. For instance, did you ever think... no, I need to take a longer run-up. You, as a person who survived Nazi concentration camps through "the trust you placed in the world"; who spent the Stalinist era in a horrific nightmare state; who—as Galley Boat-Log attests—during the decades of the Kádár regime came to know the depths of depression—did you imagine that the occupation of Hungary jokingly termed "socialism" would ever come to an end and you would regain complete personal freedom?

There's no need to take such a deep breath! In my opinion this conversation would not be worth anything if it had not become clear by now that in essence, if not explicitly, this was exactly what I was thinking of every day.

Literally?

Let's say subcutaneously so; unbrokenly in at least a tacit sense... as if something were continually prickling me.

So you weren't surprised by the change of regime?

If that's what you infer, then my answer was not good, or at least not clear enough. I lived as if the regime might come to an end at any time—and I was quite sure about that, by the way, because life will only temporarily tolerate its own denial—it was just that I couldn't be sure that I myself would live to experience it. At the time, I had a favourite saying from Kafka: "There is plenty of hope, no end of hope, only not for us."

Couldn't you find anything more reassuring?

It very much suited the daily spiritual exercises.

Would you care to relate how, as an inhabitant of Budapest, you lived through your second liberation?

Not so very differently from the first one, in Buchenwald. Liberations almost always run along much the same lines. There are certain signs, then all at once the skirmishing of struggle is picked up, then eventually, after a momentary lull, someone shouts out "We're free!"

Were you surprised? Or did you marvel at it? Or...

Both delighted and incredulous. A gigantic empire soundlessly imploded like a huge oak tree that has been eaten up inside by worms... well anyway, then the problems of survival that at first no one—myself included—had taken account of began to emerge.

Despite your seemingly inexhaustible experiences of dictatorship?

No, and I'm not ashamed to admit it, either. I am one of those childishly gullible beings who at the time democracy was restored to Hungary supposed that with the cessation of abnormal living conditions everything and everybody would suddenly be normal. As I result, I fainted from one consternation to the next: lies, hatred, racism, and stupidity erupted around me like a carbuncle that had been swelling for forty years and was finally lanced by the surgeon's scalpel.

We have already mentioned "Sworn Statement," which in

point of fact was the novella with which—how should I put it?—you took to the ring of public combat, being transformed at one fell swoop from an author of abstract novels to a public figure. I imagine that was not quite what you had in mind when you wrote the story.

Not in the least; all I wanted to do was free myself from the shame of the experience.

In any event, "Sworn Statement" burst like a bomb: already in 1991, the year when it first appeared, the actor and writer Mihály Kornis was performing it in the form of a monologue on the literary stage of the Katona Theatre in Budapest; Péter Esterházy wrote a matching novella entitled "Life & Literature," and the two novellas were soon published together in a slim printed volume, both in Hungarian and in German translation, and a bilingual cassette had also been brought out as a so-called spoken book. It may well be that you conceived it as a disaster story, but it turned out to be a decisive success story.

Yes, which crowned the misunderstanding, and on top of that, in the mirror of the political constellation of the time, it also gave an impression of the taking-up of a moral stance, which indeed it was.

Didn't you intend it to be?

If you had asked me that question then, I would have given you a different reply from the one I would now.

I'm interested in the one you would give now.

If I were to reclaim it from the topical sphere and fit it into the series of my works, then I would have to call this story the beginning of my regaining of consciousness.

Your first astonishment.

You might also see it that way.

Nevertheless, "Sworn Statement" struck me much more as a self-examination than as a piece of social criticism, as if you were probing whether the survivor of dictatorships still had enough strength to accept freedom.

Tricky question, big subject…

But the narrator of The Union Jack *poses essentially the same question, though admittedly late in the day—he has already loused up his life; there is even a touch of perverse Schadenfreude in the way he hitches his own crushing to that of his country.*

That's an unconventional reading of it…

Wrong?

On the contrary, a very empathetic one.

And a good ten years later, when the book appears, it turns out that the main characters in your novel Liquidation *are also wrestling with the same question.*

It may be the major issue of the day. People are now furtively glimpsing into the chasm—not the one that is lying there ahead of them but the one that is gaping behind them. That chasm is their own life.

Put so that's a fairly graphic image. Man struggles for his freedom, but when he wins it, or it is presented to him, he suddenly finds himself in a vacuum. Did the question as to where next never arise for you?

Of course it did, and more particularly almost vying with the pangs of "homesickness," as I could not know to what extent the pressure under which I had to live and write was of value for my works. Under healthy conditions, books like *Fatelessness* and *Fiasco* might possibly never have come into existence. If I wanted to be utterly merciless, I might say that in a dictatorship you can "enjoy" the run of the madhouse, but in a democracy a consensus exists, a genuine literary responsibility, which can restrict the profligate bent of your imagination within constraints.

Though a Kafka or a Beckett, for example, was not disturbed by freedom...

True: one can find one's prisons anywhere, but in the event that you should be wavering it does no harm to know what roots your art draws on.

Isn't that the real problem with your book Someone Else?

"Is it really just these deadly circumstances that offer me a hidden source of energy? I have no way of knowing, because the source of energy was always supplied by depicting those deadly circumstances, in the midst of those selfsame deadly circumstances," you write around the middle of the book. All the same, Someone Else *is also a novel of liberation, of gaining a wider perspective, since it is now that you make your first trips to western Europe: "with M. and I taking turns to drive and the Waldstein Sonata resounding triumphantly. . .,"* you write about a starry July 4th in 1994.

Yes, we happily zipped around the highways of Europe in a hired car.

And yet, like a hidden leitmotif, the thought unexpectedly resurfaces as an unresolved question: "Afternoon tea in the Chamonix valley. Evening was drawing in and the air was chilly. . . and fragrant. . . amid uninhabited forests, valleys and hilltops. . . With a rock for a table, we ate the Brie cheese and biscuits left over from yesterday, accompanied by a local rosé. I was freezing and M. gave me her pullover; she herself was enjoying the cool, her face was radiant. While eating we mulled over how far we still had to go and where we should stay for the night. The shadows gathered and took on ever darker hues while up on the mountain summit the trees were still in sunlight. I didn't think about it, but I suppose I was happy. It was a feeling that through a trip like this, here at the foot of Mont Blanc, my forty years of being shut in, my prison life, was attaining a fulfilment rather than becoming problematical. Arriving at the threshold of another way of living, I understood that the dividing line is so sharp, the yawning gap between the two ways of living—between myself and myself—so deep, that it can only be bridged with the most strenuous effort. It is like standing at the edge of a devastating forest fire and having to assess the losses and the gains—to assess what I have accomplished so far, and where I should look to for a source of future creative energy."

Yes, yes! A fine evening, exquisite concerns...

What do you mean "exquisite"?

Well, for instance, that we didn't have to worry about how we were going to pay for the supper.

That was already how things stood, and still you had exquisite concerns.

That's true.

It is striking that both The Union Jack *and "Sworn Statement" bear a 1991 date; Kaddish for an Unborn Child appeared in 1990, Galley Boat-Log in 1992... work was simply bubbling out from under your hand. For a while you were also a member of the editorial board of the literary magazine Holmi.[38] Then around the end of the Nineties, your name suddenly vanished from the magazine. I would have expected some kind of explanation to be given as to the reason for your parting...*

Me, too. Just to print my letter of resignation, for example, as would befit the better sort of places. Or even to inform readers how glad they were to be rid of me, or whatever. Let's move on, though.

Where to? I have a feeling we have come to a standstill, or that the high spirits are at an end. To back up to the point where, in your own words, you begin to regain consciousness and take a first look around in this new situation, your eyes immediately cloud over, if I may be permitted to extend the metaphor. You publish articles and diary entries which concern political deformations, neo-anti-Semitism, histori-cal amnesia and the like, then in 1997 you publish the book Someone Else, *which elicited widespread dislike in critical circles...*

I was drummed out of the nation like a relapsed trouble-maker from a tinpot boarding school.

But what did you do to elicit the fury of a press that, up to that point, had behaved fairly amicably toward you?

How should I know? I think you are overestimating the importance of so-called literary critics. Works of litera-ture—genuine ones, that is—lead their own lives.

That may well be, but nevertheless I'm not going to make do with that pearl of wisdom. Your speculative pieces, the essays and lectures, are almost uniformly rejected by the Hungar-ian public.

They still exist... In truth it's just the old game being carried on: I am a nuisance in Hungary, in the organic extension of the Kádár regime, a dissonant voice in a convention of self-deception which by common consent is sustained through gritted teeth.

What do you mean more precisely by "convention of self-deception"?

Keeping one's mouth shut. As a result of which the continuity of the past has been interrupted. The 1989 change in regime did not arise from the Kádár regime but arrived from "outside," from somewhere remote where real history grinds ahead. It was again necessary to adjust to the new situation, as so many times before, and that was much more urgent than looking back to see where we had come from. People supposed that the muck of the Kádár regime could be quickly scraped off the soles of our shoes. It can't, and all kinds of frustrations derive from curtailed memories. One of them is fear and self-hatred as reflected in nationalism; another is lack of direction or nostalgia for the Kádár regime. In that context, it matters little that my essays are not to the taste of superannuated literary veterans wreathed in cigar smoke on their pseudo-Olympus or of the neo-conformist careerists of university faculties who parrot the gobbledygook of literary scholarship... I myself am even less to their taste. I never asked for access to the amenities of the Hungarian intellectual and I have therefore remained an outsider...

As a tiresome stranger?

Certainly a stranger. Look, it's not just a question of my being liked or disliked but much more of how long an artistically inclined individual can maintain a creative life in discord with those around him or her... even the question of how long that may act as an inspiration, and when does the frustration arising from the dialogue of the deaf—to the point that it poses a danger to health, so to say—start to kick in.

To the extent that it may distort your power of judgment or maybe disturb the scale of values that you have elaborated so scrupulously? In your weaker moments, are you never seized by doubts or uncertainty?

Who can say they are not sometimes troubled by doubts? What I mean by that is that I always doubt every sentence I utter, but I have never for a moment doubted that I have to write what I happen to be writing. Would you believe that I am not sufficiently familiar with my own life's work? Because that probably is the case. Once I have written a book, after suffering a certain spell of remorse and nausea, I no longer know what I wrote. I never took stock of the importance of one of my works; I know nothing about that: I'm far too permeated by "the world's indifference." In this chaotic, postmodern world of ours, spiked as it is with terrorism and atrocities, I don't believe anything is of any special, let alone preeminent, importance. It seems to me that not only people but societies are not born for happiness but strife. The stated goal is always happiness, but that is always a will-o'-the-wisp. There is still no way of knowing how an individual life can be harmonized with society's goals, about which we know hardly anything. There is still no way of knowing what motivates us, or indeed, when it comes down to it, why, over and above a vegetative automatism, we live at all. Still to this day, in all truth, no light has yet been thrown on even whether *we* exist at all, or are just embodied images of the neuronal bundles at work within us—a symbol that goes through the motions, because it is bound to go through the motions, of being an autonomous reality. For me, who is of no importance, one thing which is of no importance is nevertheless important: that's more or less how it stands with literature.

These days you spend a lot of time in Berlin. What took you there?

Illness; depression; health; *joie de vivre*.

All four at once?

However odd it may sound.

Let's start with the illness.

I won't go into the physical symptoms; much more serious than those was the claustrophobic depression, which weighed my hand down like lead, locked my soul in the stocks (if it is permissible to speak of a soul as if one were talking about some kind of spinal osteoporosis, or a paralyzed limb which gives one constant

shooting pains). Around a year ago, it was so bad that I
was unable to touch the novel that was then in progress.
In plain language, I broke down.

When did that happen?

Around the autumn of 2000. At that time, Magdi, infallible diagnostician that she is, with love as her sole
implement, persuaded me that we should rent a little
"workplace" in Berlin. She realized that if I were abroad
it would be easier for me to create the inner freedom that
is a precondition for a writer. She was not wrong, either:
that turned out to be the solution, even though we had to
accept the risk of taking that step (for instance, whether
we would be able to pay the rent regularly). Later on,
the Berlin Academy of Arts awarded me a grant for a
semester, and once that had elapsed we simply stuck
around, as it were, becoming cosmopolitans, commuting
between Budapest and Berlin, indeed Chicago as well.
It was in Berlin that *Liquidation* was resuscitated; as I
walked on the Kurfürstendamm and its side streets, the
intertwining broken threads of the story appeared to me
in my imagination, the just-about-perceptible sutures
at the site of the vanished junctions like the tacking on
a coat that is turned inside out—the flimsy edifice of a
novel that was still realizable. No, I'm sorry, but please
don't interrupt me! I fear you're going to bring in the
reception in Hungary or something of the ilk that I've
already grappled with, have got over, and so is no longer
of any interest to me. You know, there are times like now,

for instance, sitting here in the Hotel Mondial, or on the café terrace of the Hotel Kempinski in the languid autumn sunshine, and absent-mindedly contemplating the late-afternoon traffic on the city's streets, under the unbroken canopy of the enormous plane trees, when for a minute or two I step out of time, and for a fleeting moment I catch myself marvelling at the adventure that my life has been.

It seems you have "drawn good profit from your sandwiches," as Laurence Sterne, that economical English writer, put it.

In that case I would much rather talk about joy than suffering. The greatest joy for me here, on this earth, was writing, language, Endre Ady and Mihály Babits, Gyula Krúdy and Dezső Szomory, the wonderful language of those and so many other good Hungarian poets and writers.

You have become a well-known, indeed world-famous, writer, the first Hungarian to win the Nobel Prize for literature. People pay attention to you, expecting words of redemption, perfection, beauty, looking for them in your works. You are girt by an aura of glory...

What are you trying to say?

Nothing in particular, I just want to quote the words of the "Old Boy" in the frame novel of Fiasco: *"I was not endowed with the redeeming word; I was not interested in perfection or beauty, not even knowing what those are. I regard no-tions of glory as the masturbation fantasies of senile old men, immortality as simply risible."* Don't you find there is a contradiction here?

Of course I do! I see contradictions at every hand, but then I take delight in contradictions.

NOTES

1. In the Mátra and Zemplén Hills, respectively, in northern Hungary.

2. An outer suburb on the NE side of Pest (part of the Sixteenth District).

3. Just off the left bank of the Danube, level with the southern end of Margaret Island (Thirteenth District).

4. Turning off the main Rákóczi Ave thoroughfare in Pest, level with what became the ghetto.

5. In the Eighth District, off the Outer (Erzsébet) Avenue.

6. The pengő was the Hungarian currency from 1927 to 1946, when it was replaced by the forint. For most of this period 1 USD = 5 pengő (though it went into the squillions per $ during the hyperinflation which followed World War II).

7. A fillér was one-hundredth of a pengő (and now of a forint), i.e., equivalent to one cent.

8. Also in the Eighth District, not far from the Grand
    Boulevard.

9. Fourth District, the northernmost area of the city.

10. The movement was used by the authorities for compul-
    sory physical training of Hungarian boys between the
    ages of twelve and twenty. It was also a way around the
    ban on regular army recruitment imposed on Hungary,
    as one of the defeated powers of the First World War, by
    the 1920 Versailles peace treaty.

11. Precise quote (Spring 1991): "I am beginning to compre-
    hend that I was held back from suicide (from the exam-
    ples of Borowski, Celan, Améry, Primo Levi, and so on)
    by a 'society' which, after the concentration camp experi-
    ence, brought me proof, in the form of so-called 'Stalin-
    ism,' that there could be no question at all of freedom,
    liberation, the great catharsis, etc.—in other words,
    everything that intellectuals, thinkers, philosophers
    not only spouted about but manifestly also believed in;
    which guaranteed me a prolongation of slave existence,
    thereby ruling out the very possibility of any such error.
    That is why I was not touched by the flood of disap-
    pointment that lapped around the feet of people living in
    freer societies, who had undergone similar experiences
    and were attempting to flee it, until gradually—despite
    the quickening of their steps—it rose up to their necks."

12. Actually *Black Sailing Ship* and anyway published in
    1958.

13. A complex metaphor for a lady of the night used by
Thomas Mann in *Doctor Faustus: The Life of the German Composer Adrian Leverkühn as Told by a Friend.*
Transl. H. T. Lowe-Porter. London: Secker & Warburg,
1949. E.g., "One such butterfly, in transparent nudity,
loving the duskiness of heavy leafage, was called *Hetæra esmeralda* [the clearwing]" (p. 14); "A brown wench
puts herself nigh me, in a little Spanish jackets, with a
big gam [i.e. shapely legs], snub nose, almond eyes, an
Esmeralda,..." (p. 142); "I saw the snub-nosed girl beside him, Hetæra esmeralda: her powdered bosoms in
Spanish bodice..." (p. 148); "...Adrian went back to that
place on account of one particular person, of her whose
touch burned on his cheek, the 'brown wench' with the
big mouth, in the little jacket, who had come up to him
at the piano and whom he called Esmeralda" (p. 154);
"The letters composing this note-cipher are: h, e, a, e, e-
flat: *hetæra esmeralda.*"

14. Imre Kertész: "Jerusalem, Jerusalem: Reflections
Sparked by the Sight of a War-torn City," *Logos* (2003),
accessible at http://www.logosjournal.com/kertesz.htm.

15. In the First District, this runs SE from approximately
Moszkva Square.

16. See entries for 1974: "Silence is truth. But a truth which
is silent, and the ones who speak up will have right on
their side."

17. See entries for the summer of 1964.

18. The nickname by which Elisabeth, the widely popular Empress of Austria from 1854 to 1898, was known.

19. From the final paragraph of *Someone Else*, included in a translation of an extensive selection of extracts published by the journal *Common Knowledge*, vol. 10, no. 2, Spring 2004, p. 314–346.

20. In the Second District of Buda, a block west of the Danube and level with the southern tip of Margaret Island.

21. See towards the very end of the entries for 1988.

22. An entry for 1966.

23. Cf. "A person always lights upon the lie he is in need of just as unerringly and just as unhesitatingly as he can unerringly and unhesitatingly light upon the truth he is in need of, should he feel any need at all of the truth…" (*The Union Jack*); "the sentences we have a need of seek us out sooner or later…" (*Kaddish for an Unborn Child*).

24. Novels by, respectively, Aleksandr Bek (1944) and Vasili Azhayev (1948).

25. *Introduction to the Method of Leonardo da Vinci* (1895), Cf. "Also lying there was a ragged, yellow-covered volume of Valéry's essay on Leonardo. He needed these for a translation he was doing" (*Liquidation*, p. 112).

26. *Drifting on the Water* (1928) in Hungarian is *Valamit visz a víz*, so a play on words can be made through the similar sounds of "*víz*" and "Weiss."

27. I.e., he had been identified as Jewish.

28. Among the entries for the summer of 1981 in *Galley Boat-Log* which is not quoted is the remark: "Good translators do not exist. This is because of the nature of the Word: you talk in your own language but you write in a foreign one" (J.-P. Sartre, *Words*. Transl. I. Cleophane. London: Penguin Books. 1967, p. 104).

29. Author's footnote: The sole exception is Sára Molnár's *Ugyanúgy téma variációi. Irónia és megszólitás Kertész Imre prózájában* [Variations on the Same Theme: Irony and Mode of Address in the Prose of Imre Kertész]; (Cluj-Kolozsvár: Koinónia, 2005), which was published just before the Hungarian manuscript of *Dossier K.* (i.e., *K. dosszié*) went to press. Sára Molnár's analyses of the texts show a profound insight, but I have not had sufficient time to ponder on her discerning evaluations with the seriousness they deserve; nevertheless, if anyone wishes to tackle my work through the route of critical analysis, this is the one book I would venture to recommend.

30. Cf. note 11.

31. Penultimate entry for 1974.

32. Cf. Scattered entries from Christmas 1963 to Summer 1968.

33. Cf. Entry for summer 1981.

34. George Orwell, *Nineteen Eighty-Four*.

35. Cf. 1964 entry in *Galley Boat-Log*.

36. Entry for August 1973.

37. "*A Holocaust mint kultúra*" [The Holocaust as Culture], a talk delivered at the University of Vienna, 1992, published in *The Exiled Language*, p.89

38. "Bits and Bobs."

WORKS REFERENCED

In English:

Fatelessness. New York: Vintage Books, 2004.

Fiasco. New York: Melville House, 2011.

Kaddish for an Unborn Child. New York: Vintage Books, 2004.

Liquidation. New York: Knopf, 2004.

The Union Jack. New York: Melville House, 2009.

In Hungarian:

A száműzött nyelv [The Exiled Language]. Budapest: Magvető Kiadó, 2001.

"Jegyzőkönyv" [Sworn Statement]. Published with "*Élet és irodalom*" [Life and Literature] by Péter Esterházy. Budapest: Magvető-Századvég, 1993.

Gályanapló [Galley Boat-Log]. Budapest: Holnap Kiadó, 1992.

Valaki más. A változás krónikája [Someone Else: A Chronicle of the Change]. Budapest: Magvető Kiadó, 1997.

ABOUT THE AUTHOR

IMRE KERTÉSZ was born in Budapest in 1929. At the age of fourteen he was imprisoned at Auschwitz and later at the Buchenwald concentration camps. Upon liberation in 1945 he worked as a journalist before being fired for not adhering to Communist party doctrine. After a brief service in the Hungarian Army, he devoted himself to writing, although as a dissident he was forced to live under Spartan circumstances. Nonetheless he stayed in Hungary after the failed 1956 uprising, continuing to write plays and fiction in near-anonymity and supporting himself by translating from the German writers such as Joseph Roth, Freud, Nietzsche, and Wittgenstein. He remained little-known until 1975, when he published his first book, *Fatelessness*, a novel about a teenage boy sent to a concentration camp. It became the first book of a trilogy that eventually included *Fiasco* and *Kaddish for an Unborn Child*. Subsequent titles include *Liquidation*, *Union Jack*, and *The Pathseeker*. He was awarded the Nobel Prize for literature in 2002 for "writing that upholds the fragile experience of the individual against the barbaric arbitrariness of history." He lives in Berlin.

TIM WILKINSON is the primary English translator of Imre Kertész (his titles include *Liquidation*, *Kaddish for an Unborn Child*, *The Pathseeker*, and *The Union Jack*) as well as numerous other significant works of Hungarian literature. His translation of Kertész's *Fatelessness* was awarded the PEN Club Translation Prize.